The ECONOMY of KINDNESS

How Kindness Transforms Your Bottom Line

Linda M. Cohen

Published by:
Aviva Publishing
Lake Placid, NY 12946
518-523-1320
www. avivapubs. com

AVIVA
PUBLISHING
New York

Address all inquiries to:
Linda Cohen Consulting
linda@lindacohenconsulting.com
www.lindacohenconsulting.com

Editing: Jane H. Maulucci, Michael LaRocca, Noelle Nightingale
Cover Design: Julie Lucas, Within Wonder
Interior Book Layout: Michelle VanGeest

On the Cover: The heart-shaped paperclip combines Cohen's themes of business and kindness.

ISBN: 978-1-63618-088-5
Library of Congress Control Number: 2021911677

Printed in the United States of America

First Edition 2021

For my husband Aaron,
my own personal Mr. Spock.
You are the logic to my whimsy.
I love our life and I love you.

Testimonials

"Sometimes it takes us too long to recognize that someone has a special ability to get us to believe in something, to tie that belief to many things that can make us better, and to suggest changes to our behavior to make it happen. Linda Cohen is a delightful storyteller who combines those elements to help understand how kindness can be the 'game changer' in business and in life."

J. J. Sorrenti, CEO Best Life Brands

"As a business leader, it's refreshing to read about a "soft skill" like kindness not only being acceptable in leadership, but actually integral in creating a great culture, retaining clients, and increasing ROI. Cohen's use of examples and stories from businesses of all sizes from the corner jewelry store to large online companies drove the point home and gave me inspiration to look for new ways to let both our team and our clients know that we truly care about their experience with us."

Pamela Mack, President, Occuscreen

"This book is a must read for leaders who are searching for the crystal ball that will help grow their business and keep their employees engaged and happy. Employees are looking for purpose and connection at work. Linda Cohen brings all of it together in this deeply meaningful book. Every organization should make this required reading for all employees!"

Brooke Jones, VP, Random Acts of Kindness Foundation

"Linda Cohen has shared so many ways and so many reasons to build a culture of kindness in our organizations. This book is an important read and an inspiration."

Susan Washington, CEO, Meals on Wheels People

"In her book, Cohen reminds us that kindness in the workplace is the true trickle down economics. Hire with an eye to a kind and caring soul, train with kind encouragement, treat your employees with understanding and empathy, and you will see them model that behavior to your customers with a genuineness and authenticity that creates a loyal following. Kindness is its own virtue, but the ROI in retention of your staff and clientele is measurable."

Pat Welch, Founder/CEO Boly Welch

"Kindness isn't just good for your soul as a human being—it's also a smart move for your business. Cohen's book, filled with heartwarming stories, highlights how kindness is critical for thriving organizations."

Kelli Harding, MD, MPH
Author of *The Rabbit Effect: Live Longer, Happier, and Healthier with the Groundbreaking Science of Kindness*

"Linda Cohen's ability to state, so simply and clearly, examples of heartwarming acts of kindness reminds me of the adage, "the best things in life are free." And to realize that practicing kindness within can lead to a happier life with its many rewards is almost too good to be true. Read this book, practice daily, and enjoy life as long as you live. If you are leading a company or a team this book becomes even more important in building a culture of peace around you."

Al Jubitz
President, Jubitz Family Foundation
Co-Founder, Rotary Action Group for Peace

Contents

"If you see what needs to be repaired and how to repair it, then you have found a piece of the world that God has left for you to complete. But if you only see what is wrong and what is ugly in the world then it is you yourself that needs repair. Not only will this make you treat each moment more precisely, but you will be more patient with yourself and with others, recognizing that there are millions of moments on the path to any worthwhile achievement."
—Rabbi Menachem Schneerson

"Do your little bit of good where you are: it's those little bits of good put together that overwhelm the world."
—Desmond Tutu

"Be kind whenever possible. It is always possible."
—Dalai Lama

"Carry out a random act of kindness, with no expectation of reward, safe in the knowledge that one day someone might do the same for you."
—Princess Diana

"Be kinder to yourself.
And then let your kindness flood the world."
—Pema Chodron

"A single act of kindness throws out roots in all directions, and the roots spring up and make new trees."
—Amelia Earhart

"Remember there's no such thing as a small act of kindness. Every act creates a ripple with no logical end."
—Scott Adams

"Kindness when given freely with no expectation in return is in fact unconditional love."
—Anonymous

Foreword

The effects of kindness are not just anecdotal. The research on the benefits of giving and receiving kindness has increased since I first started speaking publicly on this topic.

Dr. Sonja Lyubomirsky, a psychology professor at UC Riverside and the bestselling author of *The How of Happiness, The New Approach to Getting the Life You Want* researched what makes people happy. She discovered that three things impact our internal happiness. First, 50% of our internal happiness comes from your biology, your genetics, your DNA. Something none of us have any control over.[1]

Second, 10% of our internal happiness comes from our living situation, the community where we choose to live, or the people who surround you. As adults, we do have more control over this.

That left a huge piece of the pie. What else affects our internal happiness? When I ask my audiences, I often get answers like money, health or a job. Dr. Lyubomirsky determined that the last 40% of our internal happiness comes from our **intentional actions**.

For years, I have shared this with audiences because it's why I believe the **1,000 Mitzvah Project** shifted my life. It's also a fact that I want others to consider for themselves. When you engage in acts of kindness, actively looking for ways you can give more of your time, talent and perhaps treasure, each and every day it will help you live a happier life. For the past several years I've taught my three truths learned while working on the mitzvah project.

- The size of the kindness might not matter.

- There is often an unexpected ripple effect.

- Giving and receiving kindness are different gifts.

That research also syncs up with the research that the **Random Acts of Kindness Foundation (RAK)** has been sharing for years about how kindness increases our happiness. Some of the research they share includes a 2010 Harvard Business School analysis of survey data on happiness that showed doing acts of kindness also stimulates production of serotonin, aka the feel good hormone.[2]

In addition, it increases our energy and lifespan. Much of the research **RAK** uses comes from the **University of California Berkeley Greater Good Science Center** which is a continual source of data, news and articles about kindness and has been for many years.

In addition, to all that kindness increases, it has been found as well that kindness decreases our stress, anxiety and depression. The research continues to grow on the benefits of engaging in acts of kindness.

As my work began to increase with businesses and organizations, especially in the healthcare sector, I knew my programs needed more data and research, since many in my audience would consider my topic of kindness to be a "soft" skill, not a skill that actually could and would affect their bottom line. When I found the 2013 Wakefield Research sponsored by Dignity Health it proved to have some wonderful data to share with these audiences.[3]

The survey found that when people experience unkindness in a healthcare setting, a majority feel that their quality of care is negatively affected (93 percent) and many then choose to withhold information (54 percent) when speaking with their healthcare professional.

Other key findings include:

- 90 percent of Americans would feel like switching healthcare providers or physicians after receiving unkind treatment.

- 72 percent of Americans would be willing to pay more for a physician who emphasized kindness when treating patients.

- 88 percent would be willing to travel further to see a healthcare provider or physician who emphasized kindness when treating patients.

- 95 percent of Americans feel that they themselves are kind and 94 percent make a point of doing something kind for someone at least once during the week.

- However, 50 percent of Americans think children today will grow up to be less kind than their parents.

In 2019 two additional books were published that added even more data and research to the push for kindness. Those books were Stanford University professor Jamil Zaki's book *The War For Kindness* and Dr. Kelli Harding's book *The Rabbit Effect.*

At the end of 2020, a new book appeared on my radar when a colleague eagerly shared an interview she'd heard on a **Freakonomics** podcast with the two doctors who'd written it. The book titled *Compassionomics: The Revolutionary Scientific Evidence that Caring Makes a Difference* was written by Stephen Trzeciak, MD, MPH and Anthony Mazzarelli, MD, JD, MB. from Cooper University Health Care.

They share that compassion is defined by scientists as an emotional response to another's pain or suffering involving the authentic desire to help. They organized their research around a set of characteristics that make up patient-centered care including kindness, empathy, and warmth.[4]

Their research synthesized evidence that compassion in healthcare not only improves potential patient outcomes and saves money for the healthcare systems, but it also could be the antidote to the burnout epidemic for healthcare providers.[5]

It's hard to know how the global pandemic will affect our healthcare systems here in the United States as it has absolutely drained and exhausted our healthcare providers, to the point where many may actually leave the profession.

Since there is already a shortage of readily available healthcare providers in many parts of the US, this will be a challenging situation to reverse. However, around the country healthcare organizations have been working to elevate their level of kindness to retain and support their current workers and encourage others to join the healthcare profession.

I am also hopeful that perhaps somehow there will be younger people who will be inspired or motivated by the "hero" work that these frontline healthcare providers have done throughout this pandemic and might be drawn to the healthcare professions.

The research continues to evolve and is widely available to deepen the conversation I began a decade ago with organizations supporting the notion that kindness can heal, inspire, change your life and improve your bottom line.

Introduction

In January 2007, after my father's death I decided to perform 1,000 mitzvahs (acts of kindness) to do something proactive to mourn his loss. At my husband's encouragement I created a blog of the same name so I would, as he said, ". . . know when I'd completed the 1,000 acts." What had begun as a tremendously personal endeavor became a public project.

When a young Rabbi encouraged me to consider writing a book about the transformation I'd experienced by focusing on actively seeking simple and small acts of kindness, not only to mourn the loss of someone, but really as a new way to walk through the world, I laughed.

I didn't consider myself a writer at all, but that little push was enough to entertain the idea, pitch it at a writers' conference, hire a writing coach, and ultimately receive a contract from Seal Press for my first book *1,000 Mitzvahs: How Small Acts of Kindness Can Heal, Inspire, and Change Your Life,* published in 2011.

When I began promoting the book, television producers asked if I had pictures to go along with some of the examples of the kindnesses I was sharing for others to consider. There were none. Partly because it was before I had a cellphone in my pocket at all times and partly because I never thought about documenting what I was doing. I didn't have any images to share with the producers.

The year my book was published, I recorded a TEDx talk in Denver, Colorado. I began speaking about the Mitzvah Project mostly at schools, nonprofits, and houses of worship. I'd been a member of Toastmasters International for several years and found the National Speakers Association (NSA) and began learning about the business of speaking professionally.

Early on, while attending a meeting of NSA someone asked me what I spoke about and of course I replied, "Cultivating Kindness." I don't remember their exact words but they replied with something like "Oh, good luck with that." I had others in the association ask, "Who's going to pay you to talk about kindness?" or "That is never going to work." I was undeterred.

I continued to share my book and find my niche and hone my kindness message. In the meantime, I regularly followed the **Random Acts of Kindness Foundation** and learned more about the science of engaging in kindness.

In 2016, I finally stopped getting asked who was going to hire me to speak about kindness and there was an avalanche of books, posts, people and organizations whose topic was Kindness. It was pretty clear that year that people understood there was beginning to be a need for more dialogue about being kind.

Lady Gaga founded the Born This Way Foundation and Channel Kindness in 2012, but it wasn't until 2016, at the U.S. Conference of Mayors when she shared the stage with the Dalai Lama, that I believed there were even more opportunities for speaking about this topic of kindness. (Gaga's nonprofit focuses on supporting and serving young people to create a kinder and braver world.)

The Rabbit Effect by Dr. Kelli Harding and *The War For Kindness* by Professor Jamil Zaki, published in 2019, began to make me think I'd been ahead of the curve with my thinking and talking about kindness. Over the years my monthly newsletters have been filled with stories and examples of cultivating kindness even during difficult times.

Suddenly kindness was everywhere. *People Magazine* and Time Magazine both did special editions about Kindness in

2019 and 2020. It was being talked about, studied extensively and I had half a dozen speaker colleagues who were now adding kindness to their topics and specialty. No longer was anyone asking me who would pay me to talk about kindness.

My keynote in 2018 evolved into **The Economy of Kindness: How Kindness Transforms Your Bottom Line.** I was delivering it to government organizations, healthcare organizations, funeral professionals, long-term care professionals, schools, and still for synagogues and churches. The message was evolving: "Why does kindness in the workplace matter?" "What if your organization doesn't promote a culture of kindness?" "How can you be a kindness catalyst no matter what position you hold in the organization?"

There were stories in the newspapers about companies that behaved with unkindness, like the bank that fired two employees for doing the right thing because it broke company policy. (On their lunch break one of the bank employees had delivered $20 of her own money to a customer whose check had been put on hold the day before Christmas.) However, when another company read her story as part of a New York Times editorial they hired her for their credit union because they said that is exactly what they would want their employees to do for a credit union member in that position.[1]

There were stories of fellow employees going above and beyond for each other; a young nurse practitioner, a friend of our family, who delivered her son at 25 weeks, applied for standard maternity leave from her job to attend to him in the NICU (Neonatal Intensive Care Unit). Her co-workers donated 400 hours of PTO (Paid Time Off) — 10 weeks of pay, so she never missed a single paycheck.

When COVID-19 closed down our economy in March 2020, I was expecting my biggest year in my speaking business.

I had landed some national conferences scheduled for 2020 and was very excited for the opportunities to speak about kindness on bigger stages.

Since only essential workers were going out to work and the rest of us were being given stay at home orders, I followed the stories of kindness happening around the globe, instead of traveling to share my message.

Those stories were everywhere. Individuals, businesses, companies, and whole towns seemed to be uniting around a virus and spreading kindness not corona. I started calling it a kindness pandemic. If I Googled "kindness during corona" during those first few months of the pandemic, I was always likely to find a few television stations or newspapers that were sharing some wonderful kindness stories. There were heroic, monumental acts of kindness and simple ordinary actions being performed all over the globe.

CBS News Correspondent Steve Hartman launched **Kindness 101** with his three school-age children who were all hunkered down at home in western Massachusetts. He led ten Facebook Live episodes and discussed subjects like friendship, courage, honesty, compassion, and fortitude.[2]

Actor/Director/Dad John Krasinski started **SomeGoodNews** (**#SGN**) on YouTube. It ended up garnering over 2.7 million subscribers. He created nine episodes including one on prom and graduation. They were playful, fun and filled with good news happening around the world, some that he was helping to create and some that he was simply reporting on.[3]

Hilton and American Express announced 1 million hotel room nights across the United States to frontline medical professionals leading the fight against COVID-19.[4]

JetBlue announced a 'Healthcare Hero' initiative and offered 100,000 free roundtrip tickets to healthcare workers.[5]

Companies stepped up to manufacture medical supplies. Dozens of companies pivoted their manufacturing resources and began using their factories to help make masks, gowns and scrubs for medical workers. Companies like Zara, Hanes, and Gap Inc. took up the call.[6]

There were distilleries making hand sanitizer, and communities offering daily gratitude for the healthcare workers by clapping at 7 p.m. every night.

In late April, there was a 100-year-old man in the UK, who for his birthday hoped to raise £1,000 ($1,250) to support healthcare workers by walking 100 laps around his garden for charity. Dressed in a coat and tie and his military medals, his efforts wildly exceeded his goals. Capt. Tom Moore, a British World War II veteran, ultimately raised more than £32 million ($45 million). He inspired people around the world and more than 1. 5 million people donated to his cause. He was knighted in July 2020 by Queen Elizabeth II. At the age of 100, he passed away due to COVID-19 on February 2, 2021.[7]

Parade Magazine ran a segment called Resolution Kindness with 25 heartwarming stories. One of my favorite stories was about a group of high school students who created a program called Zoomers to Boomers. It's a service that delivers groceries to the elderly and immunocompromised. Within a couple of weeks, this group of high schoolers had already delivered more than 2,000 grocery orders.[8]

There was a video that went viral when a caregiver gave a D-Day Veteran a special pillow with a picture of his deceased wife. His reaction was truly heartwarming.[9]

At a restaurant in Houston, a patron left a $9,400 tip to help the owner pay his employees through the beginning months of the pandemic.[10]

Wherever I looked there were pictures and stories about kindness. Those months through the uncertainty of a Global

Pandemic also provided the hope that together we would weather this challenging time of a virus that filled us with tremendous uncertainty and fear.

The images were amazing. So much chalk art and murals, colorful pictures posted on trees, benches, walls and fences with words about love, hope, reminders to stay strong. Photos of billboards from churches or movie theatre marquees with quotes like "We're in this together, just a little further apart."

Some images that stuck out for me:

- A husband standing at the edge of an emergency room holding up a thank you sign for the healthcare workers who had saved his wife.

- A picture of two little girls pulling a wagon full of toilet paper with dolls in their other arms walking down a street.

- A grandmother standing on her balcony at a long-term care facility with her granddaughter and new husband below receiving their wedding vows.

Simple moments of one human being doing something with kindness and love for another human being.

Unfortunately, on May 25, 2020 in Minneapolis, Minnesota George Floyd was killed by a police officer with three other officers standing by, and the world shifted. The shock and disbelief that began to emerge in the white community was only the beginning of recognizing the realities people of color have had to deal with for centuries.

The protests took on a life of their own; most were peaceful but some were not. That violence and rage began to change what had felt like a "we are all in this together" kind of a moment to a time of deeper separation. I no longer saw daily kindness stories promoted by news outlets. The news had gone back to huge coverage of anger, violence, and fighting.

There were a few stories here and there in early June. One ran in the Washington Post about a 9-year-old and her friends who raised $40,000 for black-owned businesses by selling homemade bracelets. [11] But the plethora of stories about others doing kindness seemed to evaporate. And again, I knew without a doubt there were still huge amounts of kindness still happening throughout our world, it's just that the coverage and focus had shifted.

It felt in those early summer months of 2020 that everything that was broken about our society: racism, sexism, healthcare, and education discrepancies were all coming out into the public eye. There was no way to hide it under a rug and think it didn't exist. It exists very clearly and people were present to help ensure we (those of us who perhaps hadn't lived this experience) got educated and understood that there are two different experiences in this country for Americans. One for white Americans and one for people of color, LGBTQ, non-Christians, and anyone else who doesn't fit the white narrative.

In November, we were subjected to one of the most difficult election seasons anyone can ever remember. There were mean spirited debates and ad campaigns, there was a truly tremendous push to get marginalized voters to the polls and at the same time efforts to keep people from voting, and there were accusations of voter fraud and conspiracies on both sides of the political spectrum. Absolutely atrocious vitriol was spouted from individuals and parties. People were afraid of the outcome of the election assuming that no matter who won there would be nationwide ramifications of civil disobedience.

It took several days before all the states had counted their votes because of the tremendous turnout for the election and the need for mail-in ballots due to the pandemic. Finally, Joe Biden was declared the winner, but President Trump would not concede and persisted in promoting election-fraud allegations despite the absence of evidence in several post-election lawsuits.

On January 6, 2021, the day the Electoral College vote was to be ratified by Congress, Trump supporters mobbed and overtook the Capitol Building. Four people died. Many more were hospitalized. The vitriol that had been stirred up in this country was rampant. People seem to have forgotten that we are all human beings. That hate does not serve anyone and that in a democracy you certainly have a right to speak but not to do harm to others or deface property.

Fortunately, January 20, 2021 — the sunny inauguration day was remarkably uneventful. It was a day of pomp and circumstance, but activities were extremely altered because of the global pandemic. There were no inaugural balls and a virtual parade rather than a live one. After he took the oath of office, President Biden asked for a moment of silence for the 400,000 lives that had been lost since March 2020.

But the day somehow did provide a hopeful and optimistic tone for the future. Vocalists sang about the coming of a new day and hope for a future of unity. The first National Youth Poet Laureate, Amanda Gorman, stole the day when she delivered her poem titled **The Hill We Climb**. [12]

The beautiful word play delivered by this 23-year-old Harvard graduate as she stood with poise and grace before our nation provided images that were a salve to many. Another of my favorite moments was when former Presidents Barack Obama, Bill Clinton, and George W. Bush delivered a message of support to Biden and our nation, wishing the 46th President luck and encouraging all of us to move forward.

Never has kindness felt more important. We have gotten so siloed and political and vicious and nasty that I get emails and photos from colleagues and friends every week with pictures of signs being put up in businesses and windows and on lawns and billboards saying, "BE KIND!"

It's clear to me now more than ever that this conversation about the little things, starting closer to home with your neighbor or co-worker, is where this conversation must elevate. It is up to us as individuals to start a grassroots movement to reclaim what we will accept. Violence, incivility, and vitriol are unacceptable. We want and deserve respect, tolerance, civility, acceptance and kindness at the bare minimum.

I am so glad I didn't quit my work on kindness years ago when people questioned me about its validity. I know I am absolutely at the right place at the right time to help be a catalyst for a kindness movement. Each and every day, each one of us gets to choose our actions. Each day we get to choose what we do to make the world a better place, whether we've made someone feel more secure with a smile or an act of kindness as Dr. Leo Buscaglia would say. I will always choose kindness and civility and hope you will join me. Stay healthy. Be kind.

1

Culture

A CORPORATE CULTURE DEFINES the stage for the shared attitudes, values, and practices any organization puts forth for the people they employ and serve. Your employee engagement around this culture will determine how your culture gets expressed throughout your organization and to your customers and clients.

A culture of kindness encompasses so many different levels. Not only is the culture you create a standard for employees to provide an exceptional experience to the customer or client, it should also be a culture that your employees feel part of, a culture where they feel recognized, valued, a part of the team, and empowered enough to go the extra mile when needed for customers and each other.

They know that when they act on behalf of the company they will be supported. This might mean helping fellow co-workers or it might mean having the autonomy to make something right with a customer and not having to ask a manager for permission to do so.

It doesn't matter what business it is, it could be a grocery store, a tire company, a medical center or a local pizza place, when employees feel supported and part of a team they will go above and beyond to serve the customers.

Over the years of offering the **Economy of Kindness** program I have learned about large and small businesses that have successfully created cultures that encourage this autonomy. As Tony Hsieh, founder of Zappos, said, "If you get the culture right, most of the other stuff will fall into place on its own."[1]

Early on in delivering my **Economy of Kindness** keynote, I'd ask participants to share a company they loved frequenting. I learned about companies that people found provided a superior customer experience and I knew that was one important piece of a culture of kindness.

In one audience, several participants shared the story of a small pizza place that they loved because they treat both their employees and their customers like family. People don't only rave about the pizza, they rave about the kind of service they receive there. Without a doubt, in ANY audience in the Pacific Northwest where I would ask this question, participants would share a firsthand experience from Les Schwab, a tire company that was founded by Les Schwab in the mid 1950s.

Ironically on a personal note — even though there are two Les Schwab Tire stores within two miles of my home, I'd never personally been a customer — as I have a local auto shop within walking distance and had always used them. After hearing Les Schwab Tire Centers mentioned for the fifth or sixth time in an audience, I had to find out more.

The kinds of stories that participants would share were always about customer service; they'd received service out on the road when their car had broken down, they were warmly greeted when they arrived to drop off their car — employees at Les Schwab are well known to hustle out the door to greet customers in the parking lot — clients would receive service on car parts that weren't even purchased at Les Schwab. Usually there would be two or three stories per participant and others in the audience would want to share their own story with us as well.

It turns out everything about this company had been intentional. Les Schwab, who passed away in 2007, was a visionary man for his time. He knew that creating a company culture that empowered his employees and shared profits with them (half of the profits go directly back to the employees at each store) would create loyalty of both employees and community members. It has paid off in epic ways. The growth of the company, the longevity of its employees, the opportunities it provides men and women in a career path is huge. Many employees have been with the company for 30 years or more. After 68 years as a family-owned business, Les Schwab Tires was sold in September 2020 to Meritage Group. At the time of the sale, it was one of Oregon's largest companies, with nearly 500 stores in 10 states and annual sales of approximately $1.8 billion.[2] What begins as a strong culture of kindness could become a very lucrative operation in any industry.

Another company that is well known for its strong company culture is Zappos, the online shoe company. Sadly, their founder and CEO Tony Hsieh died at 46 years old in November 2020. He was revered for his vision as he grew Zappos out of his basement into a company that was ultimately sold to Amazon for $1.2 billion in 2009.[3]

The company is known for many aspects of its company culture including its month-long onboarding program. It is well known that effective onboarding helps create more engaged employees. Their onboarding provides knowledge of the company and its culture. It also allows potential employees to determine if they are a great fit. At the end of the month of onboarding, if it isn't a good fit, trainees are paid well for their long training period and there is an amicable parting.

Prospective employees who complete the onboarding program get to participate in a graduation ceremony. During this initial onboarding training program, prospective employees learn all of the Zappos cultural norms. They learn about the customer service expectations and they also learn what it means to "deliver happiness," one of the core Zappos values. Employees talk about the autonomy and independence they have while working towards the bigger goal of being a company that consistently works to meet and exceed expectations by providing "WOW!" customer service to their customers and fellow employees.

Pro Tip:

When I first began speaking to corporate audiences, I created a simple Culture of Kindness Quiz. An easy five-question quiz to ask audience members to check the temperature of their own organization.

Answer these questions for your corporate culture:

1. Does your company or organization have a system that makes it easy for customers/fellow employees to recognize a job well done?
2. Is recognition for outstanding work a standard part of your meetings or department gatherings?
3. Does your organization promote opportunities to develop everyone's full potential through mentorship/professional development?
4. Do you and your employees feel empowered to offer extra assistance to a fellow co-worker or go beyond a job title to help?
5. Do managers and team members help to create a supportive and productive work environment?

This simple quiz lets you take a bird's-eye view at some of the issues that might need a deeper dive as part of your corporate culture. There is always room for improvement with any culture but perhaps this quiz highlights some of the areas that might be worth looking into to further elevate your culture.

Whether it's professional development, recognition, mentorship, on the job training, or supportive work environments, these questions get to the heart of what your employees will want in a company with a culture of kindness. If you can't say a resounding yes to each of these questions, this would be an initial place to begin thinking about elevating your culture. Of course, changing a culture already in existence is going to require a long-term vision, buy-in from leadership, and a decision that it's an important goal for your organization.

INCLUSIVITY

It's impossible to talk about culture without addressing the intersectionality of kindness and inclusivity. Not only is inclusivity the kind way to create a company culture, it also makes good business sense.

According to a 2017 Deloitte Global Human Capital Trends report, inclusive workplaces are six times as likely to be innovative, and twice as likely to meet or exceed financial targets. The report goes on to say that while 71% of companies say they want to have an inclusive culture, only about 12% of those companies have reached what Deloitte calls the most mature level in their model.[4]

One silver lining from our 2020 experience is that companies must work to elevate their diversity and equity because consumers expect companies to share their diversity credentials publicly. It seems that chief diversity and inclusion officers are becoming more the rule than the exception in many organizations.

Perhaps many people envision what a culture of inclusivity would look like — it's all kumbaya and happiness, we love everyone, everyone is respected, and our differences are celebrated. But to really understand inclusivity we'd have to take a deeper dive to discover what *exclusivity* might be and acknowledge where we are falling down in these areas.

On the most basic level, do you have a diverse staff? Do you have ethnically diverse people (who don't look like you), do you have people who come from any other countries, religions, and backgrounds? It's perhaps easiest to be inclusive if everyone is pretty much the same. Companies that see diversity merely as checking off a box of compliance are truly missing the mark.

Diversity in a global world economy like ours is so much more than that. Each person in your organization brings to the table unique perspectives, ideas, and valuable knowledge that could be crucial in finding solutions to problems within your organization. Employees with differing world views and experiences could be seen as a huge advantage and not just satisfying a regulation.

If your culture doesn't understand the value of diversity or the actual benefits that employees who are not ethnic clones could bring to your organization, that is the first conversation that needs to take place within your company.

Second, let's say you have diversity in your staff. Next question, how do you treat your employees who are the minority, have different holidays, speak other languages, come from other places? Are they celebrated and recognized exactly the same way as your majority employees?

Before you jump to answer the question, I want you to really think about it. I have a black colleague who is a professional strategist. She works with C-Suite executives at nonprofits, government, healthcare, Human Resources, and a wide variety of other organizations. She told me that in her community of Black professionals, absolutely every single one of them can share a time when they experienced exclusivity at a job. It might have been a microaggression, but it still isn't kind behavior.

Perhaps, when John retires, after being with the company for 15 years, the company throws him a great big party with food and cards, but when Denise retires, who's also been with the company about the same amount of time, she doesn't even get a card. When Jan gets a promotion the company decorates her office to congratulate her but when Alicia also gets promoted they don't. This lack of celebration may not seem to be a huge slight but it's definitely a microaggression with unkind undertones. These are insidious ways that lack of acknowledgement can happen within a company to minority employees.

Our unconscious bias runs deep, and there are a myriad of books, training, and speakers that could help elevate the unconscious bias that might currently exist in your organization. You have to start by taking a look at your company history to see how deeply ingrained that bias is to your culture. The phrase, "We don't know what we don't know" never felt more obvious to many white people than in 2020.

This was a wakeup call to many of us that we had so much to learn about our history both locally and as a country, and uncover the uncomfortable rhetoric our preconceived notions and our thoughts and emotions have attached to these biases. Another silver lining to come out of 2020 I believe is that many, many white people began the baby steps of getting educated about systemic racism, Black history, and the biases that come with those blind spots.

Another example my colleague shared with me is the lack of collaboration. She told me about a Black speaker being invited to come in to discuss the topic of DEI (Diversity, Equity, &

Inclusion) to an organization and the planners giving the speaker carte blanche to address the group. Feeling he was the "expert" on the topic, they felt they didn't need to get involved with any of his content.

She told me, as a Black person, we want to collaborate, it's not kind for us to be having this conversation without the benefits of that collaboration. Working ahead of time to prepare together allows us to benefit from that joint experience. She said it can be very lonely to be doing the work without others' collaborative input. This is known as inadvertent exclusion.

She thought that perhaps White people are timid when it comes to the discussions about DEI because they are afraid they will get it wrong, use incorrect words or offend someone. However, the only way we will get it right is to sit down together with people who are different from ourselves to begin having these conversations.

This brings up another important point about feedback that will affect the conversation about inclusivity at your company. Who is having the conversation? If your leadership isn't diverse then it's important to include people who might not be in leadership roles but still might bring a diverse perspective to your organization.

This is one of the most valuable ways you can take the temperature of the organization. And this must be done in a sensitive way. These conversations will be difficult on many levels so go forward with kindness and perhaps even bring in someone who can help you elicit the information you need to improve. The end goal is for these conversations to provide important insight into your company culture from a diverse perspective.

To get buy-in from leadership they will have to know what their employees are experiencing, especially if it isn't their lived experience. The only way you'll get real feedback is to make sure your employees who make up this diversity are encouraged to share and are actively listened to.

Active listening will be crucial for leaders to learn what's going on in the organization. It might be a hard pill to swallow to learn that your company has many challenges around DEI. But the only way you will make changes is to know what problems you are solving. You can't fix something if you don't even know it's broken. When you start with active listening, chances are you'll know what goal or outcome you should hope to reach. Without this information you may not even be solving the right problems.

If you're not the leader and you find that there are DEI issues, you have to take the brave step and let your leadership know there has been an oversight. Understand that their behavior may not be intentional, it is more likely just ignorant; they didn't have the knowledge to do better.

Personally, I've had to raise the issue of inclusivity regarding Jewish holy days because many schools, organizations, and businesses weren't aware that the biggest holidays for the Jewish people come in the fall. Our high holidays are usually in September and October, and the dates move each year because the Hebrew calendar is based on a lunar calendar.

Over the years, at different times I've ended up letting principals, teachers, coaches, meeting planners, colleagues, bosses, and fellow volunteers know that certain dates each year won't work for annual events, meetings, back to school nights, tournaments, or other events.

Most of the time it is met with, "Oh, gosh we didn't realize, thanks for letting us know, we'll change the date" but I've also been told, "Well, it's too late there is nothing we can do about it and sorry you're out of luck to participate."

Even worse, "Since you are the only Jewish person here, it really doesn't affect enough people to make a difference so we aren't going to change the date."

There is a really simple and readily available solution to the holiday problem. If you Google "Workplace Inclusivity Calendar" you will find companies like KAZOO that have created such a calendar. If you are in a role that is planning any kind of events, it behooves you to have one of these calendars.

Moving forward, you can use these inclusivity calendars to help plan events for your organization. You can create sensitivity to important dates for others even if you don't celebrate these days with any company-wide events. Even if you don't know if you have any employees who observe these days, recognizing them on your company calendar shows one more way you are acknowledging that our world has diversity in it. And if you do have people within your organization who observe these days, your employees can support and honor each other knowing this information.

One of the most wonderful surprises that has happened over the years of my professional speaking career is the increase in colleagues who have recognized my holidays once they knew that these were important dates to me as a Jewish person. As people have gotten more aware of diversity and regular calendars include more significant dates for all religions, I often get greetings for Rosh Hashanah or Passover from colleagues who see those dates on the calendar, too.

Inclusion in a company culture provides many opportunities for kind practices to be embraced. It's certainly an area that requires active rather than passive engagement to continue to seek out your best practices.

Other ways you can be sure to create inclusivity in your work environment:

- Have employees add pronouns in their email signature. (He/Him, She/Her, They/Them)
- Provide noise-canceling headphones for offices where there is shared space.
- Create solitary spaces where introverts can recharge.
- Create ways for employees to give non-verbal feedback, such as suggestion boxes.
- Ensure all office spaces are ADA-compliant.

The end goal of creating a kinder, more inclusive organization is to help your employees feel like they belong. They belong in whatever way they show up in your company. Honestly, isn't this one of the basic premises any of us really wants, to feel like we are part of something greater than ourselves? That we belong to this group, this company, this organization. We are part of the team. It's such an important human desire.

When you create an environment of inclusivity, you allow opportunities for getting to know each other formally and informally. Formally, you could have town hall meetings or retreats, annual dinners or celebration events. Informally, cross-team activity, volunteer days, company lunches, or happy hours all provide opportunities for people to meet each other, too.

This is a conversation that requires utmost kindness as we discover that at the end of the day, no matter what our skin color, religion, or cultural background, really and truly we are all human beings, trying to live our lives in peace and harmony. When we come together, with all of our unique differences, this adds to our lives. To learn about another, someone who doesn't look or sound like you might help you understand and discover many new ways to live, to eat, to celebrate. This enriches all of our lives when we embrace diversity with love and compassion and not with fear and hate.

2

Feedback

THE VERY DEFINITION of feedback is receiving information that is the basis for improvement. When a business or organization solicits feedback, it should be for the sole purpose of improving your organization or service. However, how and to what extent this feedback is received and used varies greatly within the business world. Why would you bother to receive feedback from your employees or customers if you have no intention of changing your behavior or your culture by what you learn? Be sure that if you are going to spend the time and energy gathering the information, that you report back to your teams and address the problems presented as soon as possible.

FEEDBACK FROM YOUR CUSTOMERS

Devise a feedback platform to learn the customer's view of your service. A feedback loop is the perfect way for a company or organization to improve their services. If you don't know how your customer or client feels about your service you won't be able to learn from their experience. Depending on the type of work you do or the business you are in, feedback can absolutely make a lasting impact on an employee no matter how it's received.

As a customer, I've often been curious to know if employees get compensated or recognized in any way by the feedback I've provided and if I share negative feedback does that help the company improve their services? In more recent years, I ask the company how they use my information. It's interesting to learn that there is not one consistent way this information gets used. It ranges from doing nothing to recognizing the employee somehow, from sharing the information publicly to actual HR documentation with raises and promotions based on the feedback.

I speak a great deal to professionals who work with seniors in caregiving, long-term care associations, and other senior centered organizations. A few years ago, my client Rebecca shared with me that after her client had passed away, the client's daughter told her that one of the best parts of her mother's end of life was working with Rebecca. She had provided solace, comfort, and support at a time when it was most needed. Receiving that kind of feedback can be a heartfelt acknowledgement that you've done your job well and, in this case, had a long-lasting impact on her client. I know this recognition meant the world to Rebecca.

Unsolicited positive feedback is a simple way that you as a customer or client can share a compliment for great service with the employee, business or organization. Acknowledgement, gratitude, and kindness is always welcome.

During the early part of the COVID-19 pandemic, I decided I was going to cancel all unnecessary expenses. As I was online, preparing to cancel my Class Pass account, a live chat bot popped up and asked me if I was unhappy with their service. In our few minute exchange, she learned that I wasn't unhappy with the service, of course, I was just limiting expenses. She asked if I'd planned to use any of their services and offered an option that hadn't been listed on their website to continue my service at the lowest level but still get the benefits of the membership.

If this chatbot and I hadn't had such a positive interaction, I would have closed my account and no longer been their client. This chatbot took my feedback and provided an option I didn't think was available. Whether you have live CSRs (Customer Service Reps) or a carefully programmed chatbot, you can gather critical feedback information and provide solutions to your customers that make them feel valued.

SURVEYS FOR CUSTOMER FEEDBACK

We've all been handed a receipt at the end of a retail transaction where the employee tells us to please fill out the survey letting company XYZ know how the service was today. Filling out a survey might be just one more unimportant task on a busy day. However, surveys that are incentivized ("You'll be entered to win a gift card…") and easy ("We just have 3 questions that will take 30 seconds…") are more compelling for a customer to complete.

Eleanor Singer's research, *The Use and Effects of Incentives in Surveys*, showed some interesting findings, especially regarding incentives. The research showed that a cash incentive or a future savings is a more effective incentive than a lottery or chance to win a big prize. Prepayment incentives of $1-5 dollars increased response rates from 2-12% points over no incentives. Almost all the research showed that the incentives did not reduce the quality of the responses.[1]

When I've been speaking about kindness in the workplace, I'll ask, "How often do you go out of your way to tell a manager about the great service you received?" Most people admit they are more likely to go out of their way to report bad service than good service.

I encourage people to not only get vocal about bad service but to also share positive feedback whenever possible. I've been known to ask employees to call their manager, at the grocery store, a restaurant, a hotel, or even a retail business, so I can verbally share what that employee has done to go above and beyond their normal duties for me.

In one case, I called over a hotel manager at the end of a four-night hotel stay with my family, to give feedback about one of the front desk receptionists. He had given us exceptional customer service for all the various needs we'd had that week. The manager was happy to hear the praise for her staff. Then she asked me to please fill out a survey so that her employee would receive a $25 bonus for that written recognition. Of course, that survey was easy to fill out.

FEEDBACK FROM YOUR EMPLOYEES

360 Feedback

360 Feedback is a process of gathering (surveying) feedback from people all around the employee including the boss, peers, other employees, and sometimes clients or customers.

Well-executed 360 Feedback and using the information gathered can be a very beneficial tool for employees, but done poorly it could likely do more harm than good. Even SHRM (Society of Human Resource Management), the association for HR professionals, had a number of articles about 360 Feedback weighing the pros and cons of using it.

Some of the benefits included a wider scope of feedback that might eliminate bias from a particular manager. Another was the opportunity to bring attention to an employee's problematic behavior so that it can be resolved rather than result in termination.

However, when not delivered properly the results can hurt morale and not help it. It also takes a greater amount of time than traditional evaluations, since you are involving multiple employees in the surveys for results.

Before implementing a 360 Feedback model perhaps consider consulting a third party who is well versed in this process of feedback. With more than 30 years of experience, my colleague Karen Snyder, with Concordia Consulting, has been effectively using a 360 Feedback model to help CEOs and senior leaders who want to improve their job performance. Her process has become an effective tool for her clients. If you want positive results for your 360 Feedback program, bringing in an experienced consultant will likely provide a kinder and more beneficial outcome.

Exit Interviews

If you aren't gathering information when your employees leave your company, you are missing an important opportunity. At this ending time in a relationship with your company, asking the right questions to your departing employee could lead to insights into ways to improve your organization. Again, this must be done well, with a good interviewer. This doesn't have to be an HR professional. Even a neutral manager would work. Sometimes though an outside service might be the best option. Despite the additional expense, their expertise in gathering information could better serve your organization. You'll likely gather valuable information that might not have been obtained in other situations. When someone is leaving an organization they may embrace being honest about the company's systemic issues that they felt couldn't have been mentioned previously because of concern over the negative long-term ramifications.

Three important items about exit interviews:

1. First make it a standard part of your company process, so employees expect to go through an exit interview.

2. Second, employees' information must be treated with confidentiality unless it has to be reported for sexual harassment, criminal actions, or issues of discrimination.

3. Finally, after gathering information about the company management styles, training and pay, culture, opportunities for growth etc. be sure to compile and analyze the information. At the very least, share the results and information with upper management and leadership.

Whether it's a formal or informal interview, whether you hire an outside service to help or not, do know that the information gathered from exit interviews, if done well and utilized, just might provide insights you couldn't have gotten with other types of feedback. You may find that the information could be useful for onboarding and orientation, discover ways to improve employee satisfaction and engagement, or mentoring and other opportunities for employees to grow that will improve your company culture.

TAKE ACTION

Go ahead and solicit feedback. Use all the tools you can to determine where and how you can improve your company culture. Find creative ways to do it. Recognize your employees and your teams when they get great feedback. Use the information gleaned to provide feedback for the future. Work on solving the challenges that you learn about through feedback as well. Feedback can provide so many ways for you to elevate and support your culture of kindness.

3

Kindness In Customer Service

I HAVE BEEN FASCINATED by the way a business elevates its customer experience long before I began speaking about kindness.

How is it that some companies provide such fantastic customer service that people talk about it? Zappos, Nordstrom, REI, LL Bean, Les Schwab, and other organizations are so well known for their remarkable customer service, when I ask audiences about outstanding service, these are the names that always come up as the gold standard.

Unfortunately, it can go the other way too. No matter where I speak, the DMV (Department of Motor Vehicles) is renowned for notoriously bad service and most people have a horror story to share.

There are hundreds of books dedicated to the subject of giving incredible customer service — including former Zappos CEO Tony Hsieh's book *Delivering Happiness*. It is a keynote topic for many professional speakers and writers. There are some simple ways to think about providing one of a kind, personalized customer service and frankly I think it's an important choice for every organization that wants to be incredibly successful. It begins with how you treat your employees. Employees who are treated with kindness tend to pass along that kindness to customers and clients.

GREETING CUSTOMERS

My speaker colleague Laurie Guest is an expert in all things customer service. She's written a book called *The 10 Cent Decision: How Small Change Pays Off Big.* She teaches businesses and companies not to overlook those very tiny decisions that won't cost them a dime and will elevate their customer service in exponential ways. She believes this is what helps some companies achieve exceptional customer service.

Words matter, notes Laurie, and she encourages employers to create a simple script for their staff, one that gives the employees the basic language you'd like them to use but that can still be infused with their personality or enthusiasm.[1]

Laurie uses the example of a client asking for help in a retail store to find an item. The employee is trained that instead of just answering, "It's in aisle three," the employee is taught to respond, "I'd be happy to show you. Follow me."[2]

She goes on to say that employers often don't want to invest or spend education dollars to teach "soft skills," thinking they are somehow less valuable. But in truth, training your employees to relate to people, to make connections, to be kind and treat the client with sensitivity and compassion is really the most important part of your business. This small investment will bring your clients back again and again. Laurie suggests we start calling it an "indispensable talent" instead of soft skills.[3] I totally agree.

Consider how you feel when you enter a store and are surrounded by zealous team members that pounce as soon as you cross the threshold. Or when you enter and some disembodied voice bellows out "Welcome to XYZ, what can I help you with today?" Or when you are searching for an exact item and can't find anyone to help you, answer a question, or guide you to your purchase. Each scenario brings up a different emotion. You need to learn what works best for your ideal customer so that they feel comfortable and cared for.

If your business is one where people know exactly what they are looking for, having your capable employees to immediately greet them can be a huge benefit. Les Schwab has mastered this with what I call their "run out to the car" way of greeting their customers. I have heard dozens of stories about this customer connection and every person loved it!

People often note Nordstrom as another company that gives excellent customer service, most likely in part because their pay structure is commission based. The downside is that sometimes you end up with the overeager employee greeting, especially as you move between departments and if it happens multiple times you may feel more like you are being stalked than served.

There is definitely an art to customer service. When we apply kindness to customer service, really the bottom line is, "How would I like to be treated in this very scenario?" You'll most likely get a better understanding and develop a better customer connection.

RUNNING LATE

While patients are usually punctual to their medical appointments, it is not unusual to be left waiting for your chance to be seen in a medical office. I completely understand that emergencies happen, traffic is a problem, or an appointment runs longer than expected and that can be in a medical office or in normal life. What is needed is the kindness of information. Keep people informed.

Once, I was at a doctor's office for an appointment and the doctor was 30 minutes late. If I had just been told that from the beginning, it would have made the waiting much easier. Passing along this information is a much kinder way to treat your clients. Recognizing that my time is valuable too is my preference. It allows me to make an informed decision about rescheduling or staying and allows me to be in control of my own time rather than at the other person's whim waiting for an explanation.

Of course, there are exceptions to every scenario and emergencies do come up that can't be controlled. In these cases, it would be hard to inform the client or customer ahead of time, however, information is power. It behooves you as the business owner or company to share any information you have with your customers about the timing of their appointment or a delayed delivery of a product. Even if they are irritated at the moment, a more informed customer will likely be a happier customer in the end.

USPS CUSTOMER SERVICE

A dozen years ago, I had prepared several catalog mailings for my home-based business in a hurry. On my way to pick up the kids at school I'd gone to my local postal annex, located inside a nearby supermarket, to mail the catalogs. It was a location I frequented often because it was easy to get in and out of quickly. I dropped off my shipment and zipped off to get the kids.

Unfortunately, one of my mailings didn't have the full address on the package and the postal workers discussed what to do about it. One said just drop it in the mail and it would get returned to me. However, I had an advocate.

Over the years, I'd gotten to know one of the postal employees on a first name basis since she always worked that afternoon shift. So instead, the postal worker, who had helped me for years, decided to call me at home to let me know. Wow, how's that for two different choices of how to handle a situation! I was so grateful and thankful that when I returned to pick up the mislabeled piece, I brought a Starbucks gift card for her to say thanks.

Kindness in customer service requires that you take an extra step to treat someone as you would want to be treated. Sometimes, it's as easy as a simple phone call to provide that "Wow!" factor.

A DMV STORY

The DMV, at least where I live, is often mentioned for their notoriously bad customer service. Several years ago, when my daughter was getting her permit and driver's license, we ended up at a Portland downtown location of the DMV to get it done.

There were no appointments of course, it was just come in, take a ticket, and wait. This DMV was closest to her school so it was the easiest place for us to go on a weekday. The experience was horrific. We waited for close to an hour for her to get called to the counter to start the process. Next, she had to wait until they called her to take the computer test. After which, we waited again to get the test results — she passed — and we waited to have her eyes checked. We waited one last time until finally they took her photo for the permit. In all it was a 2½ hour procedure. Most of which was waiting to be called to complete the next part of the process.

By the time my son was ready for his permit and license, I think I'd shared that terrible DMV experience with enough other people that I learned about a DMV located in a suburb in another adjoining town. It was a 20-minute drive but the experience there was 100% different.

When we walked in we were greeted by someone who told us to take a number. Within a handful of minutes my son was called to take his permit test. He got the results less than 5 or so minutes later. The final photo taking and payment process was completed in another 10 minutes or so. In total, we were out of the DMV in less than 30 minutes.

My mind was literally blown. How could two different locations of the same organization act so completely differently? For one thing, there were more employees and there was a better flow to the process. But besides that, I can't tell you if there was inherently anything else that was different about the process. It just worked better.

The steps of the process were the same; they were just executed better. This story sincerely elevated my belief that customer service doesn't have to be terrible. With some eyes on the process and figuring out where an organization is falling down, and perhaps some customer service training for employees and managers, it's not impossible to improve the experience for your clients even at the DMV!

REMINDER CARD

In 1999, a new supermarket chain opened in Portland, Oregon. The first store that opened was located just a mile from my home. I was pregnant with my second child that year and I loved shopping there. They were certainly not the cheapest store in town but the customer service was fantastic. The employees were so helpful and empowered. The cashiers didn't need to ask their manager for a price change approval or refund, which was just one way that they personalized their connection to their customers. They grew from that initial store with only 60 employees to 17 locations with nearly 3,000 employees when they ended up selling to a bigger supermarket conglomerate in 2013.

In recent years, I learned that early on, their founder had created a wallet sized card that they gave out to all the employees as a reminder that employees and managers were encouraged to go above and beyond when helping customers. It was an actual card that they'd printed out. I'm paraphrasing but on one side of the card to the employees it said, "Do whatever it takes to help a customer." On the opposite side to the managers it said, "Say **Thank You** to your employee."

The founder wanted employees to feel safe to deliver the highest service to customers and the managers were reminded to trust and recognize those efforts, even if on occasion perhaps they disagreed with whatever action the employee had chosen to do. Several months after hearing this story, I bumped into a founding employee from my original store, who was now working at another location. I asked him about those reminder cards. He proceeded to pull out his wallet and find his now tattered card.

What may seem a little gimmicky can actually make a lasting impression on your employees and your culture.

PETERSON'S JEWELRY STORE

A few years ago, I was speaking in a very rural town in Eastern Oregon. I'd arrived in the town on a sunny spring evening about 5:30 p.m. and decided to wander down the main street to see if any shops were still open. I found Peterson's Jewelry Store.

When I walked in, I met Randall Peterson, a well-dressed older gentleman in his 80s, who took over the family business in 1959. His parents had started it in the 1920s. It was a fine little shop with several jewelry display cases down one side of the store.

Mr. Peterson and I got to chatting. He shared with me that his wife had been in the business with him for many years. Sadly, she had passed away a few years before, but he told me, when she was in the store, she would find out what the ladies of the town of Heppner wanted for Christmas. And then she would go to the jewelry shows in search of those items.

When it came time for the husbands to come in and shop for the Christmas holiday, she knew exactly what each client wanted and she had it waiting for them. He said it always worked out so well. And I realized when I heard that story, that it was simply exceptional customer service, really, really providing the client with exactly what they wanted as a holiday gift.

When I think about that personalized small town customer service Mrs. Peterson provided for the residents of Heppner, Oregon all those years it always makes me smile. And Mr. Peterson didn't do too badly himself. When I first walked in, I'd said that I was just window shopping, but after we got to chatting I mentioned I was beginning to wear my mom's gold charm bracelet and was hoping to add one or two of my own charms to it.

We ended up finding a sweet microphone in one of his catalogues. I ordered it as a Mother's Day gift to myself and have been wearing it proudly on my charm bracelet ever since. Every time I glance at it, it reminds me of Peterson's Jewelry Store and that one of a kind customer service that you remember for a very long time.

AUTOMATING YOUR CUSTOMER SERVICE

Automating your customer service with robo phone calls and chatbots online can have both a positive and negative impact. The positive is that it can be very efficient at solving minor problems or when reminding people of upcoming appointments.

My experience with the chatbot for Class Pass was very positive and efficient with an outcome being that I remained a committed customer. On the negative side, robo calls and chatbots can be very impersonal.

Several years ago, I brought my 10-year-old Toyota van in for service. Later that day, the dealership service department called to say that the vehicle needed an additional several hundred dollars' worth of maintenance. Trusting our dealer, my husband and I decided we would do all the recommended service. The service manager was very helpful, saved me a few dollars by finding some coupons to bring the cost down, and arranged for a loaner car since the work spanned two days. Overall, we'd been very happy with the service and the experience, despite the unexpected expense.

A couple of days after the service, I received an automated "thank you call" for choosing to use their service department and doing the service with their company. The recorded voice gave me a number to call if I had any further questions. Frankly, I found this very poor customer service.

If your business or organization is going to bother to make calls or send notes thanking your customers, have a real person do it! Using a robocall can actually offend your customer and make them reconsider their loyalty to you. To have an automated service calling seemed almost pitiful.

If the company really values their customers isn't it worth the investment of a real person's time to make these calls? Plus, if I did have a question, I would be speaking to a real person who could pass that information on to the appropriate department. But a recorded message? I didn't even have a chance to grab a pen for the phone number to call if I **did** have further comments.

Automation may save you time and effort but if it disconnects you from your prized customers it's likely not having the outcome you'd hoped for.

Here's how another car dealership chose to be memorable. I had an audience member share a story that resonated with simple kindness. She told me that when she brought her first Infiniti in for the initial oil change, it happened to be on her birthday. As she signed in, she provided her driver's license. She said, "Nobody mentioned anything in the morning but when I came back later in the day to pick up my car they had gotten me a birthday card and everyone had signed it." She was so moved by that simple gesture. When I asked her how many more cars she's bought since then she replied, "Four!"

Wow! I think that was a damn good ROI on that $3.99 birthday card. That birthday card created a customer for life. Of course, that was probably only one of many positive customer service interactions she's had with her dealership, but that was the one that started the relationship for her and the one shared with us during the **Economy of Kindness** workshop.

You likely know the famous quote often attributed to Maya Angelou, "I've learned that people will forget what you said, people will forget what you did, but people will never forget how you made them feel."[4]

Pro Tip:

Go out of your way to find ways to spread additional kindness for people. Keep a stash of cards around for birthdays, sympathy or get well soon. That way you will effortlessly and easily be able to jot out a message and spread a little kindness in a few minutes.

RITZ CARLTON'S 10/5 WAY

The 10/5 Way was created by the Ritz Carlton Hotels to create exceptional customer service for their guests. In an effort to extol comfort and happiness, various healthcare organizations including Ochsner Health System, a Louisiana based company, adopted this exercise in kindness in 2011.[5]

The practice is simple. Teach your employees that anytime they are within 10 feet of a guest, they should make eye contact and smile. If they are within 5 feet of a guest they should also say, "Hello."

Shawn Achor, author of *Before Happiness: The 5 Hidden Keys to Achieving Success, Spreading Happiness, and Sustaining Positive Change,* discusses this very simple behavioral shift that makes a huge difference with guests and now patients.[6]

According to Shawn Achor, "It sounds simplistic, but research has shown that these small changes can have a huge impact on customer satisfaction, employee retention, and the bottom line."

Achor shares how Ochsner formally adopted the 10/5 Way and trained more than 11,000 of their healthcare providers to use the simple technique of smiling and saying hello to patients and colleagues. Of course, there were providers who at first weren't happy to comply but soon they became the outliers, the ones who weren't following the cultural norms that were taking shape within their healthcare system.

There were skeptics, too. According to Achor, "Some of the doctors had originally had a hard time believing that something so seemingly trivial as saying hello or smiling could possibly have any real impact on health outcomes. But what those skeptics had momentarily forgotten was the scientific and direct correlation between patient satisfaction and successful health outcomes."

Ochsner reported $1. 8 billion in revenue in 2011. That year had an increase in patient satisfaction which is often the biggest predictor of profits for a healthcare system. Even a fraction of an increase on such a large revenue stream was a positive outcome for the bottom line. That certainly gave Ochsner stakeholders something to smile about.[7]

"WOW" CUSTOMER SERVICE

I first learned about Zappos after I began speaking about kindness. As an online shoe company, they instruct their call center employees to do whatever it takes to provide their customers with "WOW!" customer service. I heard one story as an example of this that has stuck with me for years.

An older woman called into the Zappos call center. She was distraught and sad and told the employee, "I bought a pair of cowboy boots for my husband a few weeks ago. He wore them once and passed away suddenly." She continued, "I'm sure it's your policy not to accept shoes for return that have been worn but I was hoping you'd consider it in this case." Not only did the employee offer her a full refund without needing to return the actual boots, the employee also sent a bouquet of flowers that arrived at the widow's house the following day.

This story surpasses customer service and truly shows empathy and kindness to another human being. It encompasses the essence of kindness that streams across your social media; "In a world where you can be anything, be kind." Or; "When you are kind to others, it not only changes you, it changes the world." To date, it's one of my absolute favorite customer service stories ever.

4

Kindness For Leaders

LEADERSHIP THAT INSTILLS kindness as part of their work protocol will have employees who feel heard, appreciated, and connected. Kindness for leaders means taking the time to pay attention to their employees and to understand and possibly eliminate their obstacles while supporting them to achieve their corporate and personal goals.

TIMELY COMMUNICATION

The pandemic was not a fair player. Time wasn't doled out evenly and many of my frontline clients talked about what kept them from being kind was their lack of time. There have been two truths during the global pandemic. Some people didn't have enough time and others had more time than they knew what to do with.

Those who were working out of the house still had the home responsibilities plus they had frontline job duties that had intensified greatly with mandatory pandemic protocols and processes that changed from day to day and week to week.

Depending on their living situation, people who were working remotely from home either found themselves isolated and restless with hours on end to fill or with not enough hours in the day to take care of their job, home, and dependents amid the chaos of confinement.

Throughout 2020 managers and supervisors, owners and CEOs took time to deliver information to their employees and acknowledge the challenges of working through the pandemic. Communicating with their employees frequently, sharing the changes that were coming to the employees whether state mandated restrictions, industry regulations, or company protocols, and getting this information to their team in a timely manner were some of the biggest kindnesses received by the employees.

This one action, taking the time to help the employees digest what they needed to know and sharing it in bite size pieces, was possibly the single best way leaders helped their organizations cope with the uncertainty and support their employees.

In the beginning of 2021, I heard a podcast from a Portland HR company called Xenium. Brandon Laws was interviewing Victoria Dew, from Dewpoint Communications, Inc. Dewpoint had completed a report called "The New Rules of Employee Experience and Communication in late 2020 and Beyond" discussing the trends they'd found in the workplace. Victoria shared that managers moving forward from the pandemic would be the linchpin of any organization. If companies and businesses could support their managers in vital ways, then that in turn would be what supports their organizations.[1]

All year long, managers, who were also going through this pandemic, were being called to support their teams. If companies were able to buoy up their managers and help them thrive during this experience, that in turn was passed along to their teams. The research showed that during the pandemic managers who had listened and communicated effectively, who asked how their employees were doing before launching into their to-do list during one-on-one meetings, helped reduce the isolation and uncertainty their employees were feeling.

Victoria noted that this could be easier for some managers than others. She suggested if managers weren't as comfortable asking more personal questions about work/life balance, they could always check in with an employee about their remote workspace, how their WiFi was functioning, if they had the access and resources they needed, or something else that would help them bridge into more personal and home life questions. This open communication could lead to other deeper needs of the employees who were truly struggling while working from their home environments.

Victoria's hope was that moving forward we'd be able to co-create solutions, that this "pandemic empowered team ownership" will help organizations discover where they go next.

I expect some of the adaptations we've made are likely to stick around when we enter the next chapter of our world, when we gain control over the virus. We will all take forward from this experience a new appreciation for our own resilience and that of our organizations, as well.

As we head forward, continue to find ways to use your time to communicate with your team in a supportive and beneficial way.

RESILIENCE

Resilience was one of the most commonly used words during 2020; along with uncertainty, pivot, change, unprecedented, and new normal. The idea of being resilient or being nimble and somehow adapting to the uncertainty that was coming our way every single day was an epic part of how people weathered the pandemic experience.

It was written about, talked about and discussed in every way possible through this tumultuous year. Companies, organizations, and individuals were called on again and again to find reserves of resilience as we weathered illness and death, shutdowns, protests, wildfires, political angst, and all the other extreme events of 2020 that made it unlike any recent time in history we may have experienced.

What did you do to call on your resilience reserves? I heard a meditation teacher encourage us to recall another challenge we had overcome in the past, something that was difficult for us but would remind us that we had resilience then and we could bring that forth to get us through this challenging year.

It didn't matter whether that previous experience was a job loss, divorce, or loss of a loved one, it just had to be some other experience that required us to build up our reserves. By recalling that experience we were reminded that somehow we weathered that experience and we will also be able to weather this one. I started thinking of it as my resilience reserves.

Companies determined to make it through this pandemic were finding resilience reserves in their own organizations. Changing their work environments in hundreds of big and small ways to make sure their businesses could stay solvent with the myriad of protocols being thrown at them.

Resilience is not easy. It takes its toll on your employees. I found that my workshop attendees were exhausted, feeling even more burnt out than during "normal" times. However, when they were supported by their managers in ways that made them feel relevant, important and that they had the support of their corporate group, they were able to keep their heads above water throughout this pandemic.

Since the beginning of the pandemic, employees and managers have been building their resilience muscle and it truly is a muscle. This experience has had us stretch it and flex it in ways none of us could have imagined previously.

My clients have said, "If you had told me in 2018 we would have our entire staff working remotely and we would still be able to function, our leadership team would have thought you were nuts." Yet, that is what we found ourselves doing in 2020 and you know what? We figured it out.

We found the resilience to get creative and discovered how to run our businesses in ways that seemed unimaginable just a few years ago. Take a minute to give yourself a pat on the back and to acknowledge that during a global pandemic, you had resilience. You and your organization have been clever and nimble, adapting and finding new methods to do something you'd never have dreamed up previously. While we wouldn't have chosen this path, it has taught us all that there are opportunities for our businesses to move forward even in chaos.

Pro Tip:

We all have the same 24 hours. Find moments, minutes during your day for a deep breath, for a grounding moment. Take the time to notice what is around you: sounds, sights, scents, and touch. In 2020, we learned just how precious life is. The more we can walk through our lives with our eyes open, being aware and present in the moment, the more likely we will be able to notice an opportunity to be kind to ourselves or others. Time passes, our lives pass, how we choose to use it each and every day is always a choice. As a leader, encourage your employees to do this as well.

AUTHENTIC LEADERSHIP

I've learned over the past decade of speaking about kindness that there has been an obvious shift that authenticity and kindness in leadership is no longer considered a weakness. In fact, it is seen more now as a strength. Leaders are being called on every day to be human, transparent, even vulnerable.

I saw an especially beautiful LinkedIn post by Lisa Cowley, CEO of Beacon Centre in the UK from October 2020. With her permission, here is the post:

• • •

"I cried at work today. On a Zoom call with a bunch of other CEOs. I cried because things felt hopeless and I didn't have my shit together and someone asked if I was ok. Do you know what happened?

It resulted in us all talking about how none of us were ok. We talked about how we have spent the last 6 months fighting to keep our organizations, our staff, volunteers and the people we support alive. We talked about how we had hit the point where it felt too difficult. The relentlessness of everything was the phrase.

Did we give up? No, we shared our worries and our sorrow and we supported each other and we will keep going.

COVID-19 is a nightmare and we are all impacted in different ways. We have all had different experiences and we have all reacted differently, but nobody hasn't been impacted.

If you are not ok, it's ok to cry. It is ok to ask for help and it's ok to want to hide under the duvet. Just don't hide forever and when you come out and talk to someone, they will surprise you and if you need someone to talk to I am here."

It really hit a chord.

The reaction was overwhelmingly positive. She received 91,000 likes and over 3,500 actual comments. Most people were encouraging, supportive, and incredibly kind. People were also really vulnerable with their own comments. As if her vulnerability allowed them to also share the scary hard stuff that was going on for them in this time of the pandemic.

When people talk about heart centered leadership, authentic, vulnerable leadership, this is the kind of CEO who is part of this movement. Someone who works every day to be transparent and respectful and kind and knows that there are so many moving parts of being a leader. A person who understands that so many human beings are relying on your leadership, insights, and support. Allowing it to be real and raw and authentic can connect and create loyalty from your employees in ways you didn't expect.

By the way, in December 2020, I saw a post from this same CEO. Apparently, her team had made her a button; it said, *"Kind But Badass."* Definitely a great mantra for leaders today to consider.

Perhaps you are familiar with Facebook COO Sheryl Sandberg whose bestselling book *Lean In* was published in 2013 about why there weren't more women in leadership. It sold over a million copies but did receive criticism from people who felt she was somewhat clueless about the struggles of average women in the workplace. That her perspective was somewhat limited and elitist.

In 2015, her husband Dave Goldberg died suddenly and I remember listening to several interviews about her second book *Option B: Facing Adversity, Building Resilience, and Finding Joy* after his death. It is about resilience and tenacity. I was impressed by her complete authenticity over the challenges of grief and loss and raising their two children.[2]

I've seen some recent articles she's been writing as well as many of the tips she shared in *Option B* that were relevant during 2020. Our life situations can certainly impact us. I have heard from more than one client who experienced a loss of a spouse, parent, or child and how that 100% changed their leadership style. Perhaps it softened them, allowed them to see that our own humanity is a shared thing. No matter our role, humans all have the same basic needs. Love, Belonging and Connection. When we acknowledge these underlying needs as leaders, there are tremendous benefits.

LET'S BE FRANK

During the pandemic, I was hired to deliver my Spreading Kindness program for my first Fire District. I'd met the incoming fire chief a couple of years earlier at a state of the union for our local town. He'd loved the idea that I spoke about kindness and we'd kept in touch about the possibility of me presenting a program to his organization.

My talk was to be delivered in mid-November 2020 while we were still socially distancing due to the pandemic. To better serve the group the program was split into two sessions. The first day, 140 fire stations would Zoom into the program, with the firefighters watching my program on a big screen from their fire stations. The second day, I would speak to the administrative day staff via Zoom, many of whom had been working remotely for months by that time.

As we neared the start of the program, I was nervous. Not only were we experiencing a pandemic, these firefighters had just come through one of the most horrific wildfire seasons anyone could remember. They were battling fires in Oregon and then joined to help their colleagues in California working nonstop for nearly three weeks. They were exhausted, overwhelmed and completely stressed.

In our preparation call, I wanted to get some "inside" kindness stories to share as part of the program, but for whatever reason, I couldn't get the kind of stories I'd hoped for ahead of time. This left me to somehow find a way to solicit these stories, in a virtual format with an audience that I'd been told wouldn't likely be very interactive.

So I tried something new, something I'd wanted to do since the pandemic but hadn't yet been ready to implement. I used an interactive online tool, where participants answer a question using a QR code that I put on the screen. This lets them be anonymous and share in real time what's really going on for them.

The question I asked was, "What holds you back from finding ways to be kind?" and there in real time almost 100 firefighters and frontline staff chimed in. Of course, time, lack of sleep, and fatigue were the most common answers. But this anonymous interaction also revealed answers like new folks, no introduction, meetings, rules that make no sense, and rough home life as additional reasons.

On the second day, I actually had a couple of fire stations that joined our program and when we got to the question, I started seeing a man's name "Frank" pop up on the screen and as the interaction went on it was growing in size meaning that more and more people were confirming that answer. I finally asked, "Who is Frank? I hope he isn't really what holds you back from finding ways to be kind."

The station that had shared his name, unmuted to tell me they were just having a little fun. That man was their fire chief and he was sitting there with them and they just loved seeing his name get bigger and bigger on the screen. We all got a good laugh about it and it completely broke through the lack of true interaction we were able to have due to the virtual format.

Later in the program, when I asked about recognition and wanted them to share something they valued that they'd received in recognition, that same firefighter shared something that Frank, their leader and chief, had given to them. It was obvious to me that these firefighters felt safe enough with their chief to be able to goof around a little, to tease him a bit but in reality, they respected him, and his leadership.

Authentic leadership doesn't have to be stiff and impersonal. As a leader, if you can relate to your teams in a truly authentic way as a real person, every part of you, vulnerable and imperfect, it will make a tremendous difference in your ability to lead others.

FLEXIBLE MINDSET

2020 surprised many people who believed that if employees weren't in their chairs at the office, there would never be the possibility that they would get their work done. Yet amidst the challenges that everyone faced with scheduling, the remote work environments, juggling coronavirus concerns, and balancing home and work life, the remote employees came through.

Many remote workers were at least as competent as they had been in the office and they were doing it despite the fears of low productivity that leaders felt before the pandemic. So what will this teach us moving forward? Hopefully, it will allow managers and leaders who had believed flexible schedules reduced productivity to reconsider that notion. It is expected that post pandemic there will be other lessons that transcend the future work setting.

One franchise owner told me that his entire staff had become remote practically overnight. By early summer of 2020, after 120 days of working remotely from their homes, they were going to resume working in their corporate home office, except on Fridays, when they'd continue to work from home. He now understood that they would be just as productive working from home as in the office.

We have taken away a great lesson from the pandemic. Productivity does not equal 40 hours in a single work setting. We've learned in fact that organizations can be run and continue to evolve, even when your employees are not clocked into a specific workspace that has been created by the company in a specific locale.

We are in the process, as I write this, of determining what the next chapter will look like for our workforces. Many organizations can leave behind the 40 hours in the office model. Others don't have a choice; their workforce must be on location to actually do the job. For the companies that can move forward to a new dynamic, perhaps the next step will be a hybrid of shared office spaces, flexible schedules or even a continuation for many employees to maintain their remote working situations.

One thing is for sure, the leadership mindset has changed. It's going to be a fascinating evolution to witness. Perhaps this is an unexpected silver lining of re-evaluating how organizations do business in the 21st century.

MENTORSHIP

Companies that have mentorship programs find that it is a win-win situation for both the employee and the employer. Mentorship, whether formally or informally organized, can have an incredible impact on your employees both personally and professionally.

According to the Association for Talent and Development, mentorship can positively affect your bottom line. Employees involved in a formal mentorship program have a 50% higher employee engagement and retention rate.[3] Even though mentoring programs have become much more common, with about 70% of Fortune 500 companies having formal mentorship programs, only about 25% of smaller companies have them.

Not only does the mentee gain insights and knowledge through a mentorship program, the organization also benefits from the investment in their employees. In an article in *Harvard Business Review*, one of the mentees, an analyst at Credit Suisse, said of her mentoring relationships, "What I learned onboarding was only 40% of what I needed to be successful. By having several key people, from staffers to VPs, assigned to me early in my career, I was able to gain the other 60% quickly."[4]

In simple terms, mentorship is just the guidance provided by another, especially an experienced person in a company or profession. Frequently, a mentor relationship can have long lasting ripple effects for both people involved. Successful leaders will almost always harken back to a mentor (or two) that helped them along their professional career path.

Mentorships are deemed most successful when this relationship is seen as a teacher to a student rather than a boss to an employee. Mentors take on the responsibility of sharing wisdom and guidance and mentees must be willing to learn. Mentees must be expected to show up, ready to do the work, and take on suggestions for professional and personal growth and development.

A mentorship requires the participants to foster honest and authentic communication. It is imperative that both parties are willing to commit the time and energy to develop and grow the relationship.

Some organizations establish a mentor peer group. This way mentors can share techniques and resources as well as send mentees to other professionals for their expertise in a certain area. This is also effective in building a broader network of reliable resources within the company by identifying the "go to" person for a specific area of knowledge.

Depending on the size of your organization and its team dynamic, you have mentoring options:

One to One — The most traditional type of mentoring is when the mentor is a more experienced person and the mentee is less experienced at the job or new to the company or department.

Peer to Peer — A team of two people in the same department or job title. One may have more experience within the company, while the other is bringing outside experience to improve or refine products or systems. They are able to exchange knowledge and offer support to each other.

Group — Several mentors work with a mentee, each sharing their particular expertise and accumulated knowledge of the company, its protocols and processes.

Another potential mentorship opportunity is when you are looking at internal advancement to leadership positions for your employees. Emerging leadership training identifies candidates for management positions and then supports them with professional development. This mentorship is provided before they are promoted so that when the right opportunity opens up, they are ready and able to step into the new role.

After a friend of mine was promoted to a management position at a major hospital in Los Angeles, she was invited to be part of a 12-week deep dive immersion leadership class. She attended with other new emerging leaders.

She noted that the organizational culture is one where professional development is encouraged. There are always opportunities for learning and development within the organization, and management is encouraged to engage in these opportunities. If she'd wanted to continue on after the 12-week program there were other opportunities to do so. She felt it grounded her for her new role in the organization as a manager. If you want your leaders to thrive this is a valuable investment opportunity.

You should also invest in your employees by sending them for further professional development outside your organization. Encourage your employees to get involved in their professional association or at the very least create a budget that pays for them to attend the regional or national conferences. Mentors can be found in an association setting. If your organization has yet to start a formal mentorship program this might allow your employee opportunities to meet someone who could serve as a mentor.

When they return, expect them to share the concepts or ideas they heard or learned that would benefit their colleagues and the organization. Again, this could take many forms but it sets up the system for professional development as well as bringing new information and ideas back to your organization on a routine basis.

As a professional speaker and a solopreneur, I have had several people along my career path who have taken me under their wing for seasons of mentorship. In some cases, it was for a short specific kind of professional mentoring and other relationships have lasted for years. I feel very fortunate to be part of the National Speakers Association that was founded on the belief that there is more than enough work for all of us and speakers don't need to feel they are in competition with one another.

By growing our speaking profession — we call it building a bigger pie — there will be even more work for all of us. So while we are all in the same business of speaking there is an incredible culture of sharing ideas, best practices, and helping each other through skill building. During the months of the pandemic when most of us were almost 100% virtual with our speaking work, a true 180 degree change from our normal onstage speaker lives, there was even more sharing, caring, and support for each other as we all adapted to these changes. I was even lucky enough to garner a couple of new special mentor relationships during this period of time.

Finally, I think it's worth mentioning Mastermind groups. While this might not be something your organization formally provides, Masterminds are a fantastic form of peer mentorship for any professional to consider.

Essentially, a Mastermind is a small group of people, I'd suggest 3 to 8 at the most, who meet in person, on the phone, or video chat on a regular basis to discuss business issues. Think of it as a sort of board of directors or a brain trust. Your Mastermind can be people who are in your same profession or different professions. Both can be incredibly helpful. There are formal Mastermind opportunities through groups like **Vistage**. There are also coaches and consultants who lead Masterminds as well. Masterminds can be life changing for entrepreneurs and managers and leaders at any level in an organization.

I created my first Mastermind when I was transitioning from a home-based business to a professional career path. To be honest, I was looking for accountability and advice to grow to my next level professionally. I formed the group by asking 3 other colleagues I knew and respected in various other businesses to come together. Two of those people invited another person. In the end we were a 6 person Mastermind. We met for almost 7 years.

Our group did morph over the years and the final group of women was not the original group we started with but over the years, these amazing women helped each other professionally and personally grow each of our businesses into very successful entities. We brainstormed, advised, asked questions, shared ideas and held each other accountable. The group consisted of a naturopath, a financial planner, a couple of entrepreneur consultants and an HR specialist. Our shared experience covered such a wide range of topics that it allowed us to look at a situation in a variety of aspects.

In more recent years, I have found that a Mastermind of speaking professionals has been exactly what I needed to grow as a businesswoman. As my speaking business grew, working with other women in my same profession provided guidance, support and accountability that was valuable at this next stage of my professional career.

One suggestion, when organizing a Mastermind group, it's helpful to find people who are at a similar level or maybe at the next level to you professionally. Formal groups like Vistage are very successful for working with business leaders and CEOs.

No matter what form of a Mastermind group works for you, the benefits of having an impartial, objective, supportive group of people who've got your back, and want you to succeed is crucial. Your Mastermind is an insightful, caring catalyst for your own professional development and they push you further by holding you accountable.

5

Communication

HOW WE COMMUNICATE, what we communicate, and how it is received are all important parts of creating kindness practices towards our employees.

During the pandemic, I'd ask employees in advance of my programs to share, "How has your CEO/manager/organization shown kindness to you during the COVID-19 pandemic?" Dozens of employees told me that the way their leaders had communicated especially in the early months of the pandemic had been the kindest action they could have offered during that time.

Especially as the pandemic began to change our world, having someone who could disseminate this information to employees in bite size, digestible and informative ways turned out to be the antidote to the chaos that was surrounding us in those moments.

Concise communication helped employees feel less overwhelmed by the changing weekly, sometimes daily procedures and protocols they were expected to follow. This allowed them to do their jobs better. Succinct communication was one way leaders showed grace and kindness through an incredibly stressful time and it was highly beneficial for employees.

These are samples of the heartfelt comments I received:

"She is a voice for our physical, emotional and spiritual needs in leadership meetings. She communicates regularly and clearly to us. She reaches out to us individually to make sure we are okay."

• • •

"Heightened communication, being available by phone, transparent about how tough it's been, encouraging self-care, timely updates."

• • •

"Our organization has shown kindness by siphoning the mass amount of information into smaller, relevant daily updates."

Others mentioned that their organization was offering spiritual and emotional caregiving to staff in the beginning months of the pandemic.

No matter what the employees shared about communication it almost always boiled down to three things.

- The leaders were communicating clearly, succinctly and compassionately.

- The leaders made time to listen to what their employees needed to succeed through the pandemic.

- The leaders provided information that was immediately relevant to their employees' daily job duties.

An added bonus was if their communication was two way. This increased employees' feeling of being listened to and cared about which was crucial as we entered the spring of 2020.

I created this graphic during the pandemic as a reminder of our communication values. Communication with our teams especially during a time of such chaos and uncertainty as in those early months when everything in our world seemed completely upside down needed to always be: Appropriate, Honest, Transparent, Beneficial.

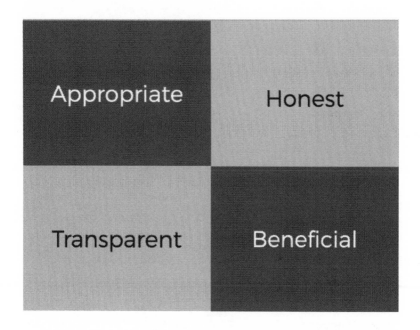

It was Arne Sorenson, CEO of the Marriott Corporation at the time of the pandemic, who inspired these concepts on employee communication during a crisis. When the pandemic arrived corporate leaders all over the world were called on to provide strength and guidance to their employees and teams.

Sorenson, who had just completed pancreatic cancer treatment and was still bald from chemotherapy, was discouraged by his board of directors to go on camera and record a video to share with his Marriott employees.[1] There was some concern that he still looked ill and that he wouldn't be the perception of leadership that the organization hoped to share. Nonetheless, he recorded a video where he told the employees the truth. The travel industry was going to be badly affected by the global pandemic, properties were likely going to be closed, and there would be people who would be laid off. His video did not sugarcoat the situation but it also provided leadership, words of comfort, and even some forward-thinking optimism about the future of their industry post-pandemic. Considering his condition, it also showed incredible courage. Sadly, Sorensen died in February 2021. He was 62 years old.

Why was communication one of the most important kindness practices of the early days of the pandemic? Having a leader share the important information that the employees needed right now took away a part of the stress that many people were feeling during those early days. Now the information was not always easy or good for sure, but if it was communicated with honesty and transparency that worked to help employees know they were in good hands.

Communication is sharing information. Especially as the pandemic began to change our world, it turned out that one of the best ways a company could be an antidote to the chaos was simply consistent and clear communication.

It was during the spring of 2020 that I heard meditation teacher Jack Kornfield share a familiar story first taught by Thich Nhat Hanh, the Vietnamese Buddhist monk. He shared that when the crowded boats of Vietnamese refugees were escaping — if they were met by pirates or storms — if everyone panicked all lives would be lost but if even one person on the boat remained unshakeable and calm, if one person held onto that inner steadiness and strength, then it was enough. It showed the way for everyone to survive and generally those boats and all of the refugees made it to safety.

The early communications from leaders to employees helped elevate a steady heart and allowed employees to remain calm in the storm of panic. This is why it became such a tremendous act of kindness to have leaders who reacted this way for their employees.

In situations throughout the pandemic leaders didn't have all the answers, they themselves were overwhelmed, unsure what the next steps might be forward. In these cases, "I don't know. . ." was an acceptable answer, and during the past year since the beginning of the pandemic we have had to accept that "*I don't know. . .*" may be the final answer for a while.

However, if the answer is "*I don't know, but with some investigation I can give you an answer...*", that is also acceptable. If an answer can be found out, just letting your employee, customer, client, patient or family know you will be looking into it further and will get back to them can put them at ease.

Taking the time to find the answer and getting back to someone will mean a great deal for the other party. They will feel listened to and heard and have peace of mind that an answer or solution will be forthcoming. Of course, during a year of pandemic there were thousands of little things that were unknown, no answer would be forthcoming without waiting and time passing. Choosing how you are direct and honest with someone when you don't know the answer can lead to a culture of trust and kindness that is invaluable.

Pro Tip:

I am not a Rotarian but I'll share something I learned through Rotary International — The Four-Way Test.

A few years ago, I had the wonderful opportunity to do some consulting work to help plant 200 Peace Poles in the Pacific Northwest with Al Jubitz, a Portland based philanthropist and decades long Rotarian. During my time doing that work, I became familiar with The Four-Way Test. This long-standing philosophy helps Rotarians internationally use and share the same language as a way to determine the proper actions in what you do, think or say. I heard it referenced many times in the months I worked with members of Rotary.

The Four-Way Test:
1. Is it the TRUTH?
2. Is it FAIR to all concerned?
3. Will it build GOODWILL and BETTER FRIENDSHIPS?
4. Will it be BENEFICIAL to all concerned?

Whether you are a Rotarian or not, I think these simple questions could be used by anyone who wants to actively evaluate their thoughts, speech, and actions. If you aren't able to say yes to all four of these questions regarding something you plan to think, say, or do, take the time to reevaluate. If more people used this simple little test we'd have a lot less thinking, doing and acting in ways that don't serve humanity.

ACTIVE LISTENING

I'm working on this one. I talk too much. Remember, I am a speaker and many speakers like myself love to talk — most of us even have stories about getting in trouble for this trait during our school days, but that's another story.

Learning to be a good listener can be one of the kindest behavioral changes you can adopt. Learning how to be fully present and employ active listening is a very important skill for both personal and professional communication. Active listening is being fully present, really focusing and listening to someone else, hearing what they say without replying, giving a solution, or even getting lost in your own thoughts about what you plan to tell them when they stop talking.

Active listening is a skill that can be developed and worked on. We have two ears and one mouth for a reason. As you know, when people talk about engaging with another human being, it isn't the speaker that people will always remember, it's the person who listened intently, invested all their attention, and was entirely present.

So how often do you really *LISTEN* to someone else? Being an active listener, especially one with a good memory, also allows you to be compassionate, have empathy, and often really connect with others in a deep and meaningful way.

A couple of years ago, while attending weekly services at our synagogue, an acquaintance inquired how my son was doing. About six months prior, he and I had a conversation about my son. Senior year had been a bit rough but when he checked in again my son was attending his freshman year at one of our state universities and was really starting to thrive in his first semester at college. The fact that this gentleman remembered and inquired about my son when he saw me after all those months actually moved me.

Why is this kind of listening so important? It allows the other person to be seen, really be seen because what you are "saying" to that other person by just listening to what they are telling you is, "*You are important. Your words are important, my time sitting here right now engaged in this experience and staying present for you is valuable.*"

Most of the time we aren't doing this. Most of the time we are distracted, thinking about or doing something else at the same time as we are "listening." When you've sat with someone who really listens to you, really hears what you said, you feel better, you feel a connection to them, you feel like your words matter.

When the gentleman at the synagogue inquired about my son, it was a touch point for me and for him a connection, a bit of humanity that crossed between us. Perhaps it doesn't sound like a lot, but this may be the one thing that we have lost with all our social media and technology. I thought about our conversation all weekend, and in remembering it to share in this chapter realized that active listening really and truly can be a simple but priceless gift of kindness we give to another human being.

Pro Tip:

Active listening takes practice. Test it out the next time you find yourself in a conversation. Make eye contact, put your phone away, pay attention to your body language and facial expressions. While listening, refrain from interrupting to offer a solution or interject an opinion unless it is requested. Be aware, you may not get to say very much, but you'll be positively memorable for being such a good listener.

6

Adaptability

THE WORD FOR 2020 FOR businesses in my mind was adaptability. In mid March 2020, when the global pandemic forced businesses to close, move their employees to entirely remote working environments or find some way to exist under the new protocols and regulations, businesses everywhere were forced to adapt.

Some threw out their regular operations and began adapting to the needs and demands that the pandemic presented. Retail fashion companies like Zara and Gap began manufacturing gowns and masks rather than clothing. JetBlue began transporting medical personnel when they saw their passenger traffic evaporate practically overnight. Distilleries all over the country began manufacturing hand sanitizer.

Initially, many companies found ways to use their infrastructure to add value for the pressing needs presented because of the pandemic. Companies that moved their staff to work offsite needed to often invest in additional equipment, furniture, and even internet hot spots to help their employees work remotely.

In my world as a professional speaker, all live engagements were cancelled like dominos in the final weeks of March 2020. Our only option was to offer virtual presentations which meant that practically overnight we needed to create home studios with decent lighting, sound and audio, and purchase equipment (much of which was back ordered in the rush to equip home offices) to be able to broadcast our programs from our own home locations. We suddenly became knowledgeable in technology as well as our content. We learned new ways to engage an audience not from a stage but from behind a computer screen. We shared ideas, insights, and best practices with our speaker colleagues so that we could all weather the pandemic.

Every business or organization was adapting. We'd been forced to find new ways to do everything we'd often taken for granted. If 2020 taught us anything it was forcing us to reconsider absolutely everything we'd ever done in business previously and perhaps more consciously choose what we'd do to keep moving forward.

Of course, all frontline workers were suddenly required to wear PPE (Personal Protective Equipment) and follow health safety protocols that changed daily. For some employees, like caregivers or hospice workers, who saw clients and families in person, figuring out how to do this effectively and safely was very challenging.

The first several months when we were trying to determine how we were going to run our businesses amid all these changes felt overwhelming. A few months into the pandemic, businesses and organizations realized this situation was likely to last significantly longer than we'd initially anticipated. This meant we were adapting constantly as we understood this new normal wasn't temporary. Over the months, we reimagined so many new ways to follow the rules and make sure our businesses were solvent in this new mostly virtual world.

In 2020, my clients taught me that creativity was the key to adapting to the changing times.

Nursing homes and long-term care facilities had to accommodate residents who were isolated from their family and friends and sequestered in their rooms. One client moved Bingo with residents to the doors of their rooms or created a beanbag toss in the hallway. They decorated carts in travel themes and rolled them through the hallways to engage residents.

One long-term care facility created elaborate decorations from various international countries like Germany, Canada and England and provided snacks from those countries for the residents. In the summer, that same facility provided a rolling farmers market cart wheeled through the halls with fresh fruits and vegetables. They taught residents to Zoom or FaceTime and created activities that the residents could participate in from their rooms or visit with their families. They created visitations with family in the summer months with outdoor distanced seating.

There were pictures of wedding nuptials taking place with a grandmother watching from the balcony of her apartment. No one thought it was perfect but these long-term care facility employees bent over backwards and worked incredibly hard to make sure residents were looked after and engaged during these very difficult circumstances.

A facility in Oregon had their residents video recorded while reading children's stories. Initially this was a project for the residents' own grandchildren but it turned out so well they shared it with their community through Facebook and on their website. It was a beautiful way for the residents to provide something that would be helpful to parents needing a little story time for their children whose lives had also been turned upside down during a global pandemic.

One of the benefits of adapting during this global pandemic was that employees and organizations tried new ideas, programs, and ways to do business. Many of these ideas will stick. This pandemic forced us to step out of our comfort zones again and again, creating new ways of doing business that may preempt and improve our pre-pandemic methods.

Through one of my clients, a Parks and Recreation association, I met Steve who was the Executive of a large Parks and Recreation department outside of Boise, Idaho. When we connected on Zoom, I saw a graphic on the wall behind him that said, "But we've always done it that way" with a huge red slash through it. He said it was a reminder to him to never stay stuck in the old way of doing something and always be willing to ask himself in any given situation, *"What can we do?"*

This was his mantra long before the pandemic. With this in mind, one of his employees came to him and wondered how they were going to pull off some of their in-person Parks and Rec events in the summer of 2020. The annual community campout would not meet the size and social distance restrictions so she came up with a new idea, to create a Backyard Campout event that would still encourage connection and participation.

She created a beautiful blueprint PDF for the event containing spooky stories with funny endings, games to play, ideas for making sweet treats and other great suggestions for this communal but individual family backyard activity. Each community member was sent a copy when they registered for the campout. The instruction booklet also encouraged people to share photos of their backyard campouts, so they could be together even while apart within their community. Registration wildly exceeded their expectations and they expect that this program might be something they add to their regular summer activities even when they are through the pandemic.

Imagining what we can still do helps us think out of the box and be creative. One side benefit of adaptability is that employees are able to take ownership of a new idea. I heard from several employees that they felt their employers were more willing to let them try a new idea during the pandemic than previously. Allowing an employee to take ownership of a project or new idea is incredibly valuable in cultivating employees' morale. Especially when the idea is a huge perhaps unexpected success.

A small Portland consulting business came up with an inventive way to help their employees with school age children, after many of those parent employees shared that they'd been struggling to balance everything. In the fall of 2020, they would turn their now empty headquarters in downtown Portland into a small school and hire a local teacher. It was a huge win-win for everyone. Productivity remained strong and the employees experienced a huge difference no longer jugging homeschooling and work responsibilities.

When employees share and discuss the most important kindness practices a company can offer it's almost always flexibility. The global pandemic forced us to adapt. It called on us to be nimble and flexible with schedules, expectations and deadlines. Perhaps one of the biggest lessons that 2020 taught us is that flexibility and adapting aren't to be feared. Suddenly, I am hearing the words from Kelly Clarkson's song, Stronger — with those lyrics, "What doesn't kill you makes you stronger." I think we all learned that lesson from 2020.

Pro Tip:

Think about your organization and the ways that you had to adapt during the pandemic. Notice the people who were the most forthcoming with ideas and innovation that helped your business.

Taking the time to reflect on the adaptations you've witnessed helps you to be more flexible in future situations.

7

Creating Mindfulness

You might not initially think that in a place of work, you can add opportunities for mindfulness for your employees. You may even question the ROI but organizations that have carved out a way to enhance the mindfulness of their employees are seeing a positive return. As we re-enter our offices post pandemic, perhaps there will be additional space available for you to consider some of these options:

MURAL MAKING

Ruby Receptionist was one of the companies I began hearing mentioned in my **Economy of Kindness** programs. They provide virtual receptionists and chat teams for all types of businesses. When I visited their headquarters in the summer of 2018, I noticed several things immediately.

Ruby's HQ had an interactive art mural in the waiting area. (Mindfulness doesn't always mean a meditation room.) There were colored pencils available so that employees and clients would add to the mural daily. It was a collective artwork in progress and a beautiful opportunity for a few minutes of mindfulness for employees and clients to engage in between activities.

THE QUIET ROOM

I visited Cascade Centers Inc., a Portland-based EAP (Employee Assistance Program), and saw a repurposed space they'd created for their employees as a quiet room. They brought in a few gently used tables, lamps and chairs and a couple of employees donated floor pillows. To enhance the space they added a water feature, artwork, blankets, a rug, candles, Himalayan salt lamp, diffuser with essential oils, meditation pillows, a portable radio and door sign. It was a huge hit with their team and helped support their employees' well-being, with a total cost less than $500! Definitely a worthwhile investment.

CARING FOR CAREGIVERS

In the spring of 2020, a hospital in California provided a "relief station" for their employees to visit during their workday breaks. It was open to all employees of the hospital. The temporary stress-relief space was filled with recorded soft music provided by their music-therapy team. Snacks and self-care products donated from grateful patients were also provided. They'd created a chalk labyrinth on the floor and as they moved through it, employees would see words of encouragement such as hope, love and peace.[1]

At the end of the walk, staff were asked to answer the question: *"What gives you hope?"* More than 100 staff shared their answers on post-it notes that were then pasted on the windows of their Child Life Room. Many of the shared answers were families, friends and their patients. But *kindness* and *my colleagues* were also answers included by several of the staff members.

The pandemic has brought to the forefront how important it is to support and nurture caregivers.

READER BOARDS

If you have a roadside reader board, you can use it for mindfulness and inspire the world. Adding thought-provoking ideas or insights that are helpful both to your employees and the world at large can be another way to have people pause and take in something meaningful for their day.

A few years ago, I passed a reader board outside of the First Unitarian Church of Beaverton, Oregon, a few miles from my home. I had to do a U-Turn to come back and snap a picture because the sign really moved me. It said: YOU GOT THIS. — God

Reader boards are a light touch with a big impact and not just for houses of worship. An automotive repair shop not far from my house has been using their reader boards for years to share inspirational messages.

I don't pass the shop very often because it's not on my usual driving routes, but EVERY single time I do pass it, I smile. They always have some relevant message that speaks to me at the moment. After my first book came out, I dropped by in person to finally say thank you and let them know how much I loved their quotes and inspirations.

A reader board communicates to everyone who sees it a little part of your company culture. It is a solid piece of real estate that can illustrate your kindness and caring for your community. Use yours to inspire others.

Pro Tip:

Mindfulness supports clarity, creativity, and calm. Consider what you can do to encourage mindfulness in your workplace.

8

Autonomy

RESEARCH FROM THE University of Birmingham, UK Business School in 2017 shows that employees who are given more autonomy in their job have increased job satisfaction. This research, published in the journal *Work and Occupations*, used data from 20,000 employees over two separate years. They theorized that due to this increased autonomy employees felt a greater sense of responsibility, pride and ownership for their own work. Autonomy has also been shown to increase motivation and happiness, along with decreasing employee turnover.[1]

Unfortunately, the research also showed that even though there are known benefits to creating autonomy for employees, in many cases managers still believe their primary role is to control and manage employees' efforts. The research also highlighted that despite the reported increased levels of well-being for employees, managers still remained unwilling to offer them greater levels of autonomy. Mainly because the manager's primary role remains one of *'control and effort extraction.'*

Autonomy is an opportunity to elevate a team's culture of kindness. When I spoke to several groups in the spring of 2020, I asked, *"What has your employer done to show kindness to you during COVID-19?"* The responses always included examples of increased autonomy in the workplace.

One participant, Jill, a Hospice volunteer manager, wrote me a very long answer to that question before our program. She shared that, as a volunteer manager, it was quite disorienting to have all her volunteers suspended as the pandemic rolled out.

Not only because coordinating them is her job, but because she said, "They are the most fantastic humans and do a large percentage of work for our hospice team." Jill continued to share that April is National Volunteer Appreciation month and the one time a year that she focuses on celebrating them.

She knew their norm of offering special recognition for them all week long, ending with a catered banquet, special speaker, and acknowledgement for years of service wasn't going to happen in 2020. Jill said her executive leadership, who valued the 75 volunteers as much as she did, cautiously agreed and allowed her to pull together a very special **Porch Project** instead.

She and her hospice colleagues created a festive gift pack that included a coupon for a free drink, designer cookies featuring their hospice logo, and a handwritten card to personally express their gratitude. They packed and wrapped each one beautifully and then a few team members helped her deliver the gift packs onto porches all over Central Oregon, a fairly large geographic area.

Jill and her masked and sanitized colleagues would place the gift at the front door, ring the doorbell and then, keeping social distance intact, would snap a picture as the volunteers stepped out to pick up the package. She said it was hard not to hug her volunteers, but she felt so grateful she'd been able to acknowledge them and scatter some joy that day.

On reflection, she told me later in a phone call that she knew she could have been laid off instead and the hospice volunteer program suspended. But her manager and the Executive Director prioritized Jill's volunteer manager role and instead allowed her the freedom to continue to nurture the incredible volunteer program.

Jill exclaimed, "To have that kind of support and trust for my idea from our Executive Director and Operations Manager, who cautiously allowed it to happen, was beyond words!"

Pro Tip:

Employees who feel empowered in their job are more likely to use creative problem solving. Their autonomy and the knowledge that management respects and supports them allows them to think beyond the standard solutions or protocols.

9

Burnout

BURNOUT IS DEFINED as exhaustion of physical or emotional strength or lack of motivation usually as a result of prolonged stress or frustration. In 2019, the World Health Organization added burnout to the official list of medical diagnoses for disease.

According to the Mayo Clinic, burnout often has multiple causes. Possible causes of burnout might include lack of control, lack of support, unclear job expectations, work/life imbalance or a dysfunctional work environment.[1]

A workplace **Burnout Survey** conducted by Deloitte in 2015 showed 77% of employees had experienced burnout at their current place of employment. The pandemic made it worse.[2]

A Medscape survey in September of 2020 showed that two thirds of doctors felt their symptoms of burnout had escalated during the pandemic. Four out of 10 doctors felt their stress level in their home life had elevated too.[3]

We have an inequity in who can work from home and who is still working onsite. Essential workers like agricultural workers, meat packers, truck drivers, and grocery store workers continued making sure our supplies and stores were still moving forward. Healthcare workers and caregivers felt the brunt of the stress as they cared for the ill and elderly.

Workplace stress is estimated to cost the U.S. economy more than $500 billion dollars a year, with lost productivity amounting to about 550 million workdays, according to the *Harvard Business Review*.[4]

Christina Maslach, a UC Berkeley psychologist who writes and studies workplace burnout extensively, says this is not a problem of the employee, it is a problem of the employer. Employers must acknowledge the situation and engage and listen to their employees to learn what the problems are that need to be fixed. It requires a long-term commitment from an organization to address the levels of burnout that exist.[5]

It's clear that burnout has become an epidemic in many professions including healthcare. As our world has begun to move at a faster pace, healthcare professionals have lost the time with patients that used to be part of the healthcare experience. Even among those at the top of their profession, many feel that the technology has made them a glorified data entry clerk, spending more time on their computers than seeing patients.

When the job becomes more about the activities surrounding the work — supervising, meetings, and management — many professionals miss the actual hands-on functions of their profession. This doesn't only pertain to healthcare professionals. This can be felt in any organization when employees move further away from the actual work they were trained to do.

This is a setup for burnout. Professionals no longer feel like their work is as valuable or meaningful.

Research shared in the book *Compassionomics: The Revolutionary Scientific Evidence that Caring Makes a Difference,* by Steve Trzeciak and Anthony Mazzarelli, shows a compelling connection between kindness and burnout reduction. Their research, gathered from data collected primarily in a healthcare setting, tested the hypothesis that compassion matters in measurable ways for patients and for those who care for the patients.[6]

Compassion is defined by scientists as an emotional response to another's pain or suffering involving the authentic desire to help. They organized their research around a set of characteristics that make up patient-centered care including kindness, empathy, and warmth. They looked at research that included the CARE Measure Survey that asks patients to answer ten questions about their care. The questions review the patient's comfort, the attention they received, and their next steps.

Their findings in the research showed that compassionate care can help reduce a patient's perception of pain. It didn't necessarily make the pain go away, it just helped ease it. They say that when a patient is shown compassion it affects their parasympathetic nervous system. This elevates oxytocin, also known as the "trust hormone." This release of endorphins while a patient and doctor are engaged in a trusted relationship helped reduce symptoms of depression and anxiety and the patient's emotional distress associated with a variety of illnesses, including cancer.

Perhaps this isn't such a surprising finding. In fact, maybe it's almost intuitive. When someone is kind, compassionate, and shows empathy towards another person we should expect to find this helps the other person's well-being. In this case, the beneficiary of that kindness is the patient and the giver is the health professional.

But, here is where their research showed some other fascinating facts that also benefited the bottom line for healthcare organizations. Patients who are treated with compassion from their doctor are more willing and likely to take their medication. This saves healthcare organizations huge amounts of money every year. Nonadherence to medical advice can lead to hundreds of billions of dollars in future healthcare expenses.

The biggest "aha" insight from their research was that compassion delivered to patients by the healthcare professional benefited the healthcare workers' *own* well-being. Perhaps that "givers high" has more benefits than we previously thought. According to Trzeciak and Mazzarelli, the evidence shows there is correlation between burnout and compassion. More compassion, lower burnout; lower compassion, higher burnout.

Elevating the compassion shown to another human being elevates that piece of humanity which is likely why these professionals got into the healthcare field in the first place, to serve and help others. When compassion is missing, it just becomes one stressful situation after another.

A climate and culture of caring and compassion serves everyone. By bringing back the human connection technology has stolen from us, burnout does not have to be inevitable. We can revamp and incorporate kindness into our labors, no matter how challenging they may be, to benefit ourselves and those we serve.

10

Being the Kindness Catalyst

*"Your people come first and if you treat them right
they'll treat the customers right."*
— Herb Kelleher

No MATTER WHAT POSITION you hold in an organization, you can be a kindness catalyst.

Let's envision four quadrants. In each quadrant, there would be a relationship between two types of people who engage with each other in business. The first quadrant is between managers or supervisors to the employees. The second quadrant would be employee to employee. The third quadrant is employees to your customers, clients, members, or whoever your business serves, and quadrant four is those same customers, clients, or members back to the employee.

MANAGER TO EMPLOYEE

Managers and leadership have a myriad of ways to promote a culture of kindness. Kindness can be shared through recognition (including understanding how your employee would like to be recognized), acknowledging and celebrating differences, mentorship, training opportunities, PTO (Paid Time Off), flexibility, fewer meetings, autonomy, engagement in problem solving, and knowing your team's dreams and goals.

Walk the halls, get to know your people, expect the most from them, help them see their potential and grow into these possibilities.

I have regularly spoken about Southwest Airlines and their incredible employee retention record. Then, I read a profile in *Southwest* magazine about their CEO Herb Kelleher who died in 2019 and I realized the incredible culture that a leader can create for an organization.[1]

It's fair to say that Herb Kelleher was a one of a kind leader. He had incredible business savvy, his tenacity to love on his employees was immeasurable, and the company under his leadership soared to heights no airline had ever experienced.

Kelleher's employees describe him with admiration, respect, and love; in fact, many people felt like he was a close friend. That's because his leadership style was people based. He loved his people and cared about them deeply. He notoriously greeted people with a hug, a laugh, and a kiss — men and women, strangers and friends. He also couldn't pass by an employee without a conversation. Many times that meant his colleagues needed to intervene so he wouldn't miss his meeting, flight, or other engagement. He didn't care. People were his business.[2] He even said, "The business of business is people."[3]

Herb insisted his employees came first and the customers were NOT always right. Empowered with the knowledge that they would be supported, employees were to treat customers well. He believed satisfied customers would become repeat loyal customers, and business would grow; and it did.

EMPLOYEE TO EMPLOYEE

If your company culture makes you feel like you are all in this together then it won't matter what role you have in the organization. You are part of a team working towards the same goal. There should be a feeling of teamwork with the understanding that we promote each other, support each other, have different styles and personalities but ultimately, no matter what our role in this organization might be, we are working towards the same outcome as one cohesive unit.

In an environment that fosters supporting each other, there are so many ways to encourage a culture of kindness from employee to employee. While ideally, leadership should be promoting the kindness culture, you can start it as a grassroots effort of cultivating a culture of kindness employee to employee.

Here are ways employees can be a catalyst:

Recognition

Recognition between employees is powerful. Your peers, more than anyone else, know what your job requires, especially fellow employees in the same or similar roles. Think of people like nurses, caregivers, first responders, or funeral directors. They understand deeply what their colleagues are experiencing.

Even if your roles are siloed in your business, your colleagues know what you add to the mix and how your efforts support the team's overall success. Being recognized by co-workers for a job well done can be a boost for the honoree and for the team to keep that positive energy flowing.

Some organizations enhance the practice of having employees recognize each other by creating ways to reward these opportunities. For example, one human resource consulting organization encourages their employees to award an *Awesomeness Card* to their fellow employee when they have gone above and beyond expectations. They can then exchange the **Awesomeness Cards** for gift cards to Starbucks, car washes, movies, or select from a collection of company swag.

Support

"You've got this!" sent by text or email, a post-it note stuck on a monitor, or a quick video or voicemail can be a huge boost when your colleague is doing something new, hard, or stepping out of their comfort zone. We are all busy but if you hear that a colleague is doing something that might benefit from them feeling supported, create a calendar reminder for yourself and then reach out. I have heard from both the recipient and the giver of this kind of support over the years and in that moment, receiving support from a peer can help a colleague tremendously. It always feels so much better to know we are in this together.

Personal Acknowledgement

All of us have a life outside of our jobs and that life includes celebrations and disappointments. It is a kindness to find ways to support and recognize your colleagues through these ups and downs. Good news could be anything from a milestone birthday to a hard earned degree. It is up to the person sharing the news how far and deep they want it to be shared and celebrated. The same goes for bad news which could be that milestone birthday or the loss of a loved one. Whatever the news is, be kind in how you share the news and support your co-worker and consider the impact on the rest of the team as well.

You may wish to involve your co-workers in something as simple as a group card or floral delivery or more detailed such as setting up a meal train or arranging for a celebratory meal. Not every person will want their personal situations shared, so your biggest kindness is respecting their wishes.

Active Listening

Active Listening is often mentioned as the single most kind thing one employee can do for another.

When a colleague is having a hard day at work, having someone to listen to them, with no judgement just a kind ear might be all they need. This is an act of kindness that seems small but can have a big impact. Allowing your fellow employee to unload a little and be heard can often make a huge difference. Depending on the day and the circumstances it's likely we will both be the talker and the listener with our co-workers.

Even if your organization does not have a kindness culture, you can still influence your immediate colleagues or team. Think of it as planting seeds of kindness that will take root and spread as a grassroots effort through your company. Your efforts may get top leadership to make a cultural change, and at the very least you have set a standard for kindness for the people around you.

EMPLOYEE TO CUSTOMER

No matter what profession you are in, please realize that you are the expert in that field of work. You are the resource, the experienced person who has gone through this hundreds of times, you have the opportunity with any customer you touch to share what you know. As a firefighter or funeral director, workforce professional or nurse, when someone engages with you, any guidance you provide them about their situation will have that much more weight coming from you.

As your customer or client, your patient or your resident, we are looking to you to help us see our way through this often challenging experience. No matter how routine or normal this becomes for you because it is the work you do every day, understand that most people have never been in this situation before and they are relying on your professional expertise. Always remember this and it will elevate the way you do your work and make you even better at connecting with the people you serve.

I keynoted my first Funeral Directors Association Conference after my mother had taken her life with an overdose of medication in July of 2014. In my speech, I shared the story of my experience of arranging a funeral while deeply grieving.

• • •

My mother had wanted to be cremated and my stepfather wanted to honor her wishes. When my stepfather, husband, and I sat in the funeral home to talk about the final arrangements, we discussed urns and money. I remember very little about a ceremony or rituals that begin the grieving process. We were given little guidance. Since my mother hadn't practiced Judaism that wasn't considered much as part of the equation.

My stepfather did agree to a service at the Unitarian church where my mother had attended frequently and I arranged the details, even asking our congregational Rabbi to come and provide a few words. Six months after my mother's death, my stepfather and I had a falling out when I inquired about her will.

He had told me previously that we would plant my mother's ashes at some point but that never occurred. He remarried soon afterwards and the ashes remained in his home. I felt ungrounded having no physical memorial to visit for my mother. I had learned with the death of my father, that rituals around death are important to help with the grieving process.

In the fall of 2018, I hatched a plan. I was working on a peace pole project with a local Rotarian and would plant a memorial peace pole on the grounds of the Unitarian church. They loved the idea. My stepsister, brother, husband and I laughed and told stories about my mom that October day when we planted the peace pole. It had taken several years, but I finally felt some closure after my mother's death.

When I added this story to share at the funeral directors conference, I knew it resonated. I implored the funeral directors to recognize that each family they sit with is experiencing this loss for the first time. As experts in their field, families are benefitting from their expertise and knowledge.

I'd never heard of a scatter garden or other possible ways to place ashes for someone who is cremated. I had only ever really known about burial in a cemetery. Perhaps some additional guidance upfront would have allowed us to have some additional choices with my mother's ashes.

Additionally, I suggested they consider a follow up phone call six months or a year later, especially when a death has occurred in a tragic way like suicide, to provide additional compassion and guidance for those who are grieving.

No matter what profession you are in, even if this work you do is routine to you, your expertise and guidance is absolutely crucial for those you serve.

Since you are an expert in your field, find ways to ask key questions so that you can more fully understand the needs, wants, and concerns of your customer or client. They will feel that you are connecting with them on a human level and don't just see them as a paycheck.

The toughest communication is when you fail to deliver the product, service, or experience as expected. Something went wrong and it may very well be on your end. Be courageous when faced with these challenges and find out what went wrong. This next story shows the power of being authentic and kind with your customers, especially when circumstances affect your best ability to give great customer service.

• • •

In February 2020, I read about Dumpling Week in the local paper. This has been a Portland tradition for the past 7 years. Restaurants create special menus to encourage customers to order dumplings (and other items from their restaurant). We'd never participated, but I thought, "Why not? Let's do it!" After perusing the nearly two dozen options we decided to order from a restaurant called Boke Bowl, even though they were located across town, because they could accommodate all our dietary needs including gluten free.

I ordered online and got a 6:30 p.m. pickup time. I drove across town and called as suggested when I arrived to get my curbside pickup. I was told they were running late and it would be another 20 minutes. When I called back the second time, I was told it would be 20 more minutes. I could tell they were busy because there were lots of people waiting on the sidewalk while I waited in my car.

I did eventually get my order almost an hour late. When I spoke to the server the third time, I attempted to be kind. It's a global pandemic, I thought, it's a special week for them, give them grace I said to myself, but I WAS kind of irritated. I said, "Do you think you'll be able to knock a few bucks off the order for us tonight?" She told me her manager would be going through the orders and would be in touch.

Luckily, the food was delicious.

Three days later, when the leftovers were all gone and I'd practically forgotten about the wait during Dumpling Week. I got an email, but it wasn't just for me.

The manager started by acknowledging our experience. She said that they'd "Spent the last 36 hours scouring orders from that night and hunted down your email address in case you were a victim of the chaos."

Then she sincerely apologized. "First off, we are incredibly sorry for the inconvenience. . . It was awful and we acknowledge it and are so sorry at how it ended up."

Then she shared that, "While we were prepared and excited for what we usually experience during this week, we were NOT able to keep up with the nearly 100 orders that came in during the hour you ordered or had scheduled your pickup. We are not trying to make excuses, but to put the night in context we've never EVER seen more business in one hour in the 10-year history of Boke Bowl."

Then she asked for our forgiveness. "We hope you'll consider giving us another shot and would love to further discuss and hopefully make anything right for you if you are still upset."

It was brilliant! I felt seen, heard, acknowledged. I actually sent the manager a reply and thanked her for her kind email acknowledgement and told her we'd definitely give them another shot, probably post COVID restrictions so we could actually eat there next time.

She was so happy to get my reply that she sent me a $20 gift certificate!

Customers want to be acknowledged. This email recognized my pain and apologized for it. I probably would have given them another shot anyway because their food was really delicious. However, receiving the apologetic email and a gift certificate certainly made me want to travel across town to give them a second chance. It makes them distinctive. They've gone to a level most businesses wouldn't bother to rise to, and for that they stand out in my book. Will I give them another shot? Absolutely!

CUSTOMER TO EMPLOYEE

Easy Feedback

Every business that directly interacts with the public needs a mechanism to give managers feedback from their customers. By putting comment cards on your retail service counter, or on the table in the restaurant, or tucked inside the check presenter, you make it simple and easy for customers to let you know when your employee has gone above and beyond in service. Having this information empowers you to recognize your outstanding employees.

When I get exceptional service, I always want to tell the manager. I encourage you to do the same. We know it is easy to complain and many people only give negative feedback, so let's turn that around by letting management know when the service is outstanding.

• • •

When our kids were small, we visited my in-laws in Boca Raton, Florida. Since their car couldn't accommodate the six of us while we were there, we arranged to rent a van beginning on the second day of our trip. At 9 a.m. that morning, I received a call from the car rental agency that the van had been delayed and probably wouldn't be ready until about 1 p.m.

Since she'd let us know we changed our plans for the morning. While we were having lunch she'd called again to tell me that they still hadn't gotten our car in and it would be likely 4 p.m. before we could come get it. It was a little disappointing, but again we decided what to do and ended up taking the kids to the pool in the complex for a wonderful afternoon of swimming.

At 3 p.m., I received a third call that our car had arrived and would be available for a 4 p.m. pickup. When we got to the rental agency and took care of the paperwork, I asked the rental agent, who I'd been speaking with all day, if I could speak to her manager. By the look on her face I knew she was thinking I was going to complain.

Quite the opposite! I told her manager that even though the delay had been a small inconvenience, the consistent communication from her employee had made it not only tolerable but satisfactory. Her communication took a situation that would have been frustrating and irritating and transformed it into just an inconvenience. This allowed us to have control on what we would do with our time during the delays.

I know the employee didn't expect this feedback and I was glad to be able to applaud her handling of a difficult situation. Her kind actions actually improved the experience tremendously.

Tips

Tipping wait staff is the most appreciated form of *acknowledging great service*. I worked as a waitress through college at a kosher deli, the Concord Hotel in the Catskills, and a fancy suburban restaurant. I know the value of a tip received for good service.

• • •

In 1985, when I was 17 years old, I landed a housekeeping job at the Black River Inn on Main Street in Ludlow, Vermont, population 2000. This is the ski resort town where my family lived for nearly two decades.

My pay was $3.25/hour. I won't say I loved the work. It was hard and somewhat repetitive. But jobs were hard to come by in those days so I stuck with it. About two months into the job, in room 214 there on the wooden dresser were three crisp one dollar bills and a note someone had handwritten that just said, "Thank You."

I have never forgotten how it felt to receive that. It's what reminds me every single time we travel for business or pleasure to do the same for the housekeeping staff. Perhaps after COVID-19 we will consider these essential workers more with the kindness and love they all deserve.

11

Reputation

THESE DAYS NO ONE can escape being scrutinized for their actions. For years, I've talked about Reputation as one of the Three **R's** (Reputation, Recruitment, Retention) of why kindness is so crucial in the workplace. Every day you can find stories of businesses and individuals whose reputations have been impacted as the result of monstrously unkind actions.

Social media has completely changed the landscape for controlling negative PR for an organization or an individual. In the past, if something negative occurred within your business realm the injured party might share it with their close circles of influence within shouting distance, or through a phone call. Now if they share it with their network it will be blasted online and shared literally worldwide to potentially thousands of people who will not have the benefit of knowing that there may be another side to the story.

The best way to maintain a positive reputation is to always be kind and honest. Mistakes will still happen and how you respond to those errors will impact your reputation and your bottom line. Be responsive to negative situations, clean up the mess as quickly as possible, and keep your client/the public informed about your actions to rectify a bad situation.

UBER

In the summer of 2017, a story broke that Uber CEO Travis Kalanick had been asked to resign from the company. During the previous months there had been a series of scandals about sexual harassment involving Kalanick.

He'd been described as creating the behemoth company through his macho leadership style and had recently lost some senior executives. The last straw was when several videos of Kalanick yelling and cursing at Uber drivers about rates went viral. At that time, the board of directors requested his resignation. Even though he had been at the helm of Uber for years, it was clear that his leadership style would actually harm the company moving forward.[1]

To replace Kalanick, the board of directors chose CEO Dara Khosrowshahi, who had a completely different leadership style to his predecessor. In August of 2017, when he was introduced to the company, he came in and listened. There was a tremendous amount of work to undo the issues facing the company and people needed their chance to be heard. He crowdsourced what employees thought the cultural norms should be at Uber and after listening to what employees were telling him, Khosrowshahi created a new culture norms manifesto.[2]

He believed since it had come from the bottom up, employees would buy into it since they helped shape it. He was right. One of my favorite norms is "We do the right thing. Period." After Uber had experienced years of a leader who had done anything but this, now they were seeing a completely different type of leader at the helm.[3]

A year later, when asked how things were going, Khosrowshahi told the reporter, "The new norms have slowly but surely spread positive change across the company." He added in an email to the reporter, "For culture change to take hold at a big company, it can't come from the top down."[4]

When I began sharing the Uber story, I would often ask if anyone had stopped their Uber ridership as a result of what was going on at the company that summer. Many people would raise their hands, and state that they had begun using other ride sharing companies.

My daughter was actually the first source I had for this story when my husband and I visited her in Seattle in October 2017. Normally, we would take the train between Portland and Seattle and then use Uber to get around the city with her. When we arrived on this trip, she shared all the allegations that were facing the Uber CEO with us and said she and several of her 20-year-old friends had dropped Uber and were using Lyft instead.

You may think that's a small group, but let's consider that they are college students — a key market for Uber, and are social media savvy. What Uber decides to do with their dollars and their messaging to make sure they win their market back can have long-term ramifications for the company.

This is a crucial step to a company's bottom line to fix the problem AND to communicate their solutions.

U.S. BANK

On Christmas Eve in 2019, Emily James, a senior banker at a U.S. Bank call center in Portland, Oregon was trying to help a bank customer whose $1,000 paycheck had been placed on hold until it could be verified. They'd been on the phone for more than an hour and the hold on his check meant he couldn't access the funds, meaning he was essentially broke before Christmas.

The customer was calling from a gas station. It was 3:30 p.m. and he'd been unable to even put $20 of gas in the car to get home. With her supervisor's approval, Emily drove 14 miles to the gas station, stepped out of her car and handed the customer gas money, wished him a "Merry Christmas," and then went right back to work.

A week later on New Year's Eve, the regional service manager was waiting for Emily when she arrived at work and fired her because of this unauthorized interaction with a customer. Her supervisor was also fired.

When the Oregonian newspaper originally published the story, U.S. Bank stood by their decision. It wasn't until a month later after Nicholas Kristof, a New York Times columnist, published a scathing article that U.S. Bank began revising their first statement and started apologizing for their actions.

The bank offered to re-hire their former employees. In the end, Emily took another job with a credit union in California. The credit union's human resources manager shared in the press that instead of firing an employee of theirs who'd done a similar act of kindness around the same time, they had given her a reward. He felt Emily James would be a great fit for their organization.[5]

In February of that year, U.S. Bank posted a statement on their website that said they were committed to learning from their mistakes, evaluating all of their policies, and making sure they are flexible enough to put the customer first while ensuring the safety of their employees.[6]

If you believe reputation is important for the bottom line of your company then Uber's motto: "We do the right thing. Period." is one more businesses should embrace.

12

Recruitment

IN NOVEMBER 2020, we lost a true visionary when Tony Hsieh, the former CEO of Zappos, died over Thanksgiving weekend. He stated, "If you get the culture right, most of the other stuff will fall into place on its own."[1]

Zappos never seemed to struggle with recruitment. In fact, there is some Zappos' folklore that it's harder to get a job at Zappos than it is to get into Harvard University.

Every organization would like to have that problem of too many applicants and not enough positions. Fields such as healthcare, long-term care, and the funeral professions struggle to find people willing to take on this challenging but rewarding work. Recruitment becomes easier with a culture of kindness in place and by doing two things — storytelling and courting recruits.

STORYTELLING

Learn to tell the story behind the job. Storytelling is powerful because it gives an insider's view of the work and it brings the role to life better than a job description that lists tasks and responsibilities. The stories expand the view of what it is like to be part of your work and mission.

Your stories should answer key questions: What keeps my employees committed to their work? What do they love about working in our organization? What kindness has our team shown to our clients? How do we show kindness to our employees, especially during difficult times?

The answers to these questions come back as heartfelt stories that show dedication, commitment, and compassion. One story told to me was from employees applauding their leadership for deciding that communicating with and listening to their clients was more important than performance during the early months of the pandemic.

What about you, how are you telling your stories? You have control over the powerful stories that get shared. People who hear your stories may be drawn to your organization once they understand that they could be part of a meaningful, valuable profession featuring a work environment that supports them as a whole person.

While preparing for a keynote program for franchise owners of ComForCare, I spoke to Alma, one of their caregivers. She had worked in the profession for years but had a very specific story she shared about working with a challenging client.

Alma's client suffered from dementia and sometimes this woman was extremely difficult. One night while Alma was sleeping the client called the police to the house to declare that she was bitten all over. Their investigation proved that was untrue. The police then called the client's son and he calmed his mother and told her he would be over the next day. When he arrived he immediately apologized to Alma for his mother's behavior.

Alma told me, you need incredible support especially when you have clients with dementia. She worked together with the family to support their mom. She also had a boss who would make time to listen whenever she needed to talk about tough situations. The combination of a supportive boss and understanding family members was very important. She felt like she was a crucial part of the team.

Alma said, "I was with that client for three years until she passed away. It makes me feel good in my heart, to know that I have helped someone."

This is the type of story you want to tell when you are looking for new employees. A story that shows the truth of the labor and the benefits of doing the work.

Become a storyteller. Tell the incredible stories about your profession, your people, and the benefits you offer for both your clients and your employees. These stories are what people will remember. It's how we are wired. We won't necessarily remember the data or statistics, but a good powerful story sticks.

COURTING RECRUITS

When you are recruiting, think of it as courting. You are in competition with all the other opportunities presented to your potential hire and you have to show them why working for your organization is the best decision. You want to show yourself authentically and highlight the best attributes of your company and the employees who work there. When a candidate applies, you might have to woo them a little to ensure that they know you are interested in them.

For example, caregivers are in short supply and can be more selective about their employment. They may be applying to more than one agency and you'll need to convince them that you are their best option.

Do a little handholding by confirming all appointments, sending a thank you note after the interview, and having the owner give them a follow up call. These actions will set you apart as a company that cares. By showing your commitment to them as a recruit, you are educating them about your company culture and you are making them take notice of you with your persistence.

My daughter recently began a job with a Portland based human resources company. Their communication throughout the recruitment process was exceptional. She was told at every step in the process what the next step would be. By the time the interview process was complete she really wanted the job. She says it harkened back to her days in customer service at Nordstrom, under promise and over deliver. Her experience now as an employee of the company is indicative of their company culture. She continues to be treated with kindness and respect just as she was in the recruitment process.

WHO DO YOU KNOW?

When searching for great new hires, look to your current team. It is likely that you have an excellent employee who has someone in their circle that is looking for a new opportunity. Since your employees are the best ones to talk about the work they do and the environment they work in, your prospect will have insider information before coming to the first interview. Plus, you'll have your employee pulling for the company and the prospect to make a match.

Employee recruitment recognition programs can inspire your team to find your next hire. Determine what motivates your team; a financial incentive, a personal acknowledgement, or a special luncheon or dinner. It's expensive to find, hire, and train a new employee. This is one way to actually reduce some of that time and expense by having the prospect come to you fully aware of the company culture, expectations, and mission.

TARGET MARKET

Can you picture your ideal employee? Just as you design an avatar for your perfect client, you should create another for who you want to employ. Consider their ideal attitudes and aptitudes and then reach out to your community to find them. Take the time to participate in career days at the local high schools, colleges, and job fairs. These are great ways to make your company top of mind and lead you to finding just the right person or people you're looking for. Plus, it makes you visible in your community and spurs more knowledge of and connection to your business. The pandemic left many people looking for new opportunities and employers vying for the new hires. In situations like this you need to be ready to tell your story to share the work you do, the culture you provide, and the opportunities that potential employees will have working in your organization.

Think out of the box and elevate how you treat employees, how you recruit new talent, and perhaps you'll become the Zappos of employee retention for your industry.

13

Retention

*"Train people well enough so they can leave,
treat them well enough so they don't want to."*
— Richard Branson

RETENTION MIGHT SEEM like a tricky thing. People leave jobs for all kinds of reasons: change in life situation, career advancement, more money, but one reason you never want someone to leave your place of work is because it's an unkind place of employment. When you develop a mindset where everyone knows that we all succeed together, that when you help anyone you help everyone, that your company encourages individuals to grow and evolve, your employees will want to stay. With a healthy company culture, if your employees **must** leave it will not be as an angry and disgruntled person.

Strong retention policies build a strong bottom line. It costs vast sums of money to replace a current employee. The costs of recruitment include advertising, HR hours for selection and interviewing, time lost with an empty position, training and onboarding the new person, and the disruption to the company of losing the employee and then bringing in a newbie.

Older statistics say on average it costs 21% of an employee's salary to find a replacement.[1] Recent statistics from **The Society for Human Resource Management (SHRM)** estimate that the average replacement cost of a salaried employee earning $60,000 per year might be close to $30,000 up to $45,000 in recruiting and training costs.[2] Those statistics and numbers don't even take into account things like employee morale, lost customer relationships, or other inherent knowledge that leaves with your former employee. It can also take a great deal of time to get a new hire up to speed to be a productive part of the team.

It is up to your managers to have a pulse on what's happening with their employees. They need to understand how the workload, protocols, processes, and unit functionality is wearing on your employees so they are prepared when an employee announces they are leaving.

Consider these questions from your employees' point of view:

- Does the company best utilize my skill and talents?
- Does the company appreciate my work?
- Does the company empower me?
- Does the company environment focus on kindness and respect?

These might be simple questions but if retention is an issue it might be time to start asking them.

Retention of exceptional employees can make a huge difference in a culture. As Richard Branson said, make it hard for your employees to leave by creating an exceptional company culture.

Prior to the pandemic, Southwest Airlines had an extraordinary retention rate, especially in the airline industry. Southwest had an average employee turnover rate of 2.5% in an industry where those rates are significantly higher.[3] They stand out. They also are proud that they've never had a layoff since beginning their business in 1973 and anticipated avoiding pandemic related layoffs.[4] With the lowest ticket prices, the company still ranks at the top in customer service and safety. Clearly their culture is one that sets them apart in more ways than one.

HOME FOR THE HOLIDAYS

As the keynote speaker at a women's leadership event for a major grocery/retail chain, I addressed 250 women—with only three men in the audience: the CEO and two vice presidents. During my program, I asked the participants to share with each other a time when they had received kindness from a manager or fellow employee. After a few minutes, I looked for two volunteers to share their stories with the entire group.

One woman told the audience that her boss had extended an act of kindness about 10 years earlier that she had never forgotten. Just three days before Christmas, her boss called her into his office. She was young, in her twenties, and she had been living in a different state far away from her family for about five and a half months. She was feeling very sad to be spending her first holidays alone.

As an act of kindness her manager announced that he was giving her Christmas week off. Then he said to her, "Buy a ticket. I want you to go home and please don't come back until after the new year." He was paying for the ticket as well since he knew the cost would be another obstacle to her traveling.

In the retail business, this is an incredibly unusual opportunity because we all know it's all hands on deck for holiday shopping. When she shared this story with our group, her boss was one of the three men in the audience. He and the rest of us got to relive this joyous memory that she still carries with her years later.

You never know the kindness that you do for an employee, how it's going to stay with them, how they're going to remember it, how they're going to think about it. I can assure you, when we all heard this story shared live there was not a dry eye in that audience, knowing that she was getting to thank him publicly now years later.

Imagine how it felt for her to be recognized and acknowledged as a valuable member of the company, so valuable in fact that it was more important for her to have time with her family at the holidays than working in retail. Think of how that company culture was created to allow that manager the autonomy to provide that kindness. Now, think about how your kindness might ripple out for your employees and co-workers.

RETAINING LONG-TERM CARE GIVERS

In the fall of 2020, Zack Demopoulos, the owner of a ComForCare franchise in New Jersey, told me that almost as soon as the pandemic began, he decided to do something each Monday for his 40 caregivers. Normally, a staff member or a nurse would drop off PPE to the caregivers; instead, using all the precautions, he started doing it himself.

Zack would meet them outside in parking lots or driveways in the rain, snow or sun, before they headed to their clients and handed out their essential supplies. At the same time, he would thank them for being brave caregivers and front-line heroes during this crisis where their clients needed them more than ever. He told them that while he knew that this was their job, they needed to know that it was so much more than that. It was a lifesaving and compassionate responsibility they did so well.

On a weekly basis, Zack grew so much appreciation for what they did that he would add a little more support in the form of a small gift, like a hand sanitizer or a bottle of water. At least every couple of weeks, he brought them lunch, even getting their specific preferences since many of them wanted to eat healthy choices. While the office had always acknowledged birthdays by mailing a greeting with a gift card, Zack now delivered them personally. He also made a point to be available to listen to them, never being in a rush, asking them if there was anything he could do for them, and always thanking them for what they did.

He had a large team of caregivers in his organization and he said it was definitely an investment of time but one more valuable than anything else he could think of doing as it pertains to taking care of his employees. Zack also said by October 2020 when we spoke, that he'd never felt so gratified. He felt like he was connecting better than ever with his staff even though he had been operating successfully for over twelve years. He said he would likely keep it up as the months continued.

He also told me that many of his other peer franchisors were struggling with caregivers quitting during the pandemic. Zack had only lost four employees and he felt his high retention rate was largely due to the relationships he built just by showing up each week.

Zack believes that visiting these front-line workers, his caregivers, in the field, bringing them a small token of appreciation, or just visiting and listening to their needs became one of his most important jobs of 2020.

To retain the employees you already have in your organization: show up, listen and let them know they are an integral part of your organization. Help them feel valued and appreciated for the dedication and effort they are putting in to do their job and serve your clients.

Pro Tip:

7 Simple ways to retain staff:

1. Ensure you're hiring right — evaluate motivations and interests during the interview process

2. Address people by name

3. Provide professional development opportunities

4. Encourage teamwork and build systems to support it

5. Clearly define work expectations

6. Make employee recognition a company value

7. Allow flexibility and autonomy

14

Team Building

HONORING DIVERSITY IN your organization actually leads to some very rich and important conversations. It can foster connections between people who may be dismissive or disinterested or unaware.

> *Always remember that you are absolutely unique.*
> *Just like everyone else.*
> –Unknown Author[1]

There are many reasons people list to identify how they are different from other people. The world and the workplace is filled with different generations, different backgrounds, different cultures, and different experiences. When this is seen as a positive and it is cultivated the truth will emerge that while we may *seem* different there are so many ways that we are the same.

GENERATIONAL CONVERGENCE

A funeral director and the president of several funeral homes reached out to me just before the pandemic began because his employees were having generational challenges working together. There was often underlying tension among the three generational groups and the president was hoping I could facilitate an honest conversation about it in a safe space. Before I met with his employees he gave me some background on each group.

The Baby Boomers (1946-1964) were a bit inflexible to changing the ways they wanted to work because, "we've always done it that way." While they were a very vocal minority, they were a little stubborn and possibly a bit stuck in some of the old patterns and routines.

The challenges he was having with the much larger group of Generation X (1965-1980) and Millennial (1981-1996) employees was their different work ethics and their new ideas for getting the work done.

The two younger groups were also tuned in to the evolving funeral profession and they had thoughts on creating updated rituals for the funeral process. (According to the National Funeral Directors Association the trend for cremation has been steadily on the rise and in 2015, the rate of cremation exceeded that of burial.)[2] The Gen Xers and the Millennials had noted that traditions needed to evolve as more people opted out of the more common funeral process including a viewing, a religious service, a grave and burial.

The first thing I asked the group to do was rearrange themselves into groups sitting with their own generation. This in itself was telling. The group of Boomers was seven people. They were all sitting at one round banquet table. The Millennials and Generation X were about eight or nine tables' worth of people, so approximately 50 employees. Next came the discussion questions:

- What are the strengths of your generation?

- How do we motivate you?

- What makes you like coming to work?

This prompted a very fruitful discussion. Each group shared several recommendations when we talked about expectations of their boss, all agreeing that they wanted to work for someone who sets clear expectations, is a good listener, and is honest and supportive.

When we discussed the strengths of each generation, the younger generation shared they are technologically savvy and innovative. They feel like they are trend setters. The Boomers said their strength was wisdom and experience and being financially responsible.

One attendee shared the realization that as part of a younger generation that grew up in such an instantaneous world, they expect everything to happen quickly. He was realizing in real time that perhaps when they have a question or need advice, it might not always be something they can get answered on the spot, especially if it requires a conversation with a Boomer. He recognized it might be better to schedule a time for a more in depth discussion.

Many of the Boomers mentioned that they would enjoy providing guidance and mentorship. They were feeling like the underutilized, old guard, not up with the trends, and concerned that they would say or do the wrong thing when working with their younger colleagues. This opportunity to clear the air and to engage honestly with the younger generation in a safe way was very helpful.

As they talked to each other, I could see the light bulb go off for some of them as they mentioned what they brought to the organization and then realized, instead of clashing about their differences and techniques to get the job done, they could coexist and actually leverage and lean into each other's strengths.

I was grateful to help them have some of those "aha" insights during our time together. A few days later the president of the funeral homes sent me an email which said, "Watching the interaction and engagement of our team was so encouraging. Your team building exercises were so successful in understanding our differences. Days after the event, there was still a buzz going around."

COMMON INTERESTS

Other ideas for team building include reading a book, watching a movie or documentary, listening to a podcast and then discussing the topic and how it applies to their organization. When the employees have a shared collective experience and can discuss ideas, resolve situations and create solutions, this creates a deep and rich culture that can transcend the workplace.

By bringing your team together for an open dialog from a shared experience, whether it is playing baseball or reading a book, you create a highway for communication and understanding. Intentionally cultivating shared experiences can be a win-win for your employees and your organization. They become a community with a common language and ideally a willingness to be more objective and open with each other.

15

Legacy

LIKE PLANTING A TREE, a legacy is what you do now to provide for someone in the future. A legacy is something you leave behind, some effect you had on others, your space, your community, your world.

Face it, maybe you haven't even thought about your legacy. But each and every day of your life you have an opportunity to create it; with your interactions, your choices, and your actions.

In 2017, I was asked to keynote for a female only service organization called Altrusa International. Altrusa was founded in 1917 more than a decade after Rotary International was founded in 1905 and more than seven decades before Rotary would officially invite women to be part of their organization. The crazy thing was I had **never** even heard of Altrusa though I was very familiar with so many of the other membership-based service organizations like Rotary, Lions, Kiwanis, and Shriners.

It was the 100th anniversary of the organization and this district conference was focusing on their legacy. Membership service organizations overall have struggled in recent decades to gain new younger membership. Most of these organizations have aged in place and the memberships now largely include mostly retired people.

Unfortunately, for many of these groups the declining membership was based on thinking younger people lack the desire to serve their communities. This isn't the whole story. The truth is, the economy has had a tremendous effect on free time and community involvement since a household now requires multiple incomes to survive. This more than a lack of desire impacts the amount of free time younger generations can commit to above and beyond their family.

Altrusa, like other service organizations, needed to find ways to adapt and change and still serve their community if they wanted to continue. Unfortunately, as I prepared for the Altrusa program I found that there was a deep and sadly held belief that change was bad. It almost seemed like they were holding on to the ways the organization was designed in the past but not acknowledging the impending disaster of their organization if they didn't adapt to changing times.

I was charged with helping this conclave envision what their legacy might be, what inviting and changing with the times might mean for their organization. Allowing them to reflect on *the skills they'd learned, the friendships they'd made, the community they'd created* and reminding them how valuable this had been.

Encouraging them to realize that by choosing not to adapt to changing times, this would all be lost and a younger generation might not have that opportunity. Rather than be threatened by these changes and new perspectives being brought to them by younger members, they would be able to serve as mentors, to help envision, and to grow a new generation of leaders to carry the torch forward of their beloved organization. Legacy is seeing change as an important part of evolution and often the only option for survival. Fresh ideas and perspectives are always necessary to create any kind of a lasting legacy.

The best part was that I was able to use their stories of kindness to help illustrate the possibilities for the future. We shared dozens of stories of Altrusa members involved in kindness towards each other to imagine all that was possible and could be gained from participation in this fabulous organization.

I shared this quote that day, since it spoke to me and this message of legacy that I was hoping to express.

"Your beliefs become your thoughts.
Your thoughts become your words.
Your words become your actions.
Your actions become your habits.
Your habits become your values and
Your values become your destiny."
–Unknown[1]

MY PERSONAL LEGACY

My kids had been part of a unique summer arts camp called Willowbrook in a suburb of Portland, Oregon. It was founded by a woman who had envisioned children learning art, music and theatre in a day camp setting with free choice and a huge amount of autonomy. The camp began in her backyard.

By the time my daughter was old enough to attend her first year, the camp had grown immensely. The camp was now erected each summer in a town park (a two-week process that up until that time the founder's son in law had largely done by himself with a skeleton crew). The registration topped 1,000 campers each week for the six weeks of the camp. The founder was no longer the director. One of her daughters had taken on that role. The board of directors was made up of friends of the founder.

After my kids had attended the camp for half a dozen years, it was clear we were Willowbrook devotees, scheduling our entire summer so our kids could attend all six weeks of camp. That summer, two of the board members, now friends, asked if I would serve on the board of directors. There had yet to be a board member who wasn't hand selected by the founder.

I heartily agreed and began my six years of service on the board.

A legacy doesn't have to have colossal impact, it can be small changes, but changes that might help move things forward in an organization. My legacy with Willowbrook as part of the board included envisioning and initiating new ideas for both our fundraising and our annual action, recruiting several other new board members over the years (one who went on to serve as president of the board), and participating in a strategic planning committee to evolve from a family-owned entity to one that could sustain itself beyond the family's involvement.

I was always grateful that those two leaders saw something in me that could be beneficial to the organization. My legacy is a part of that camp. It allowed me an opportunity to spread my wings and use my skills at a time when I needed that. And I believe I helped in moving the camp forward at a time when there were some serious challenges facing it. Allowing an organization to morph and grow and change to evolve to the times is incredibly important. Legacy is both about an organization and the individuals who serve it.

16

Connection

ONE OF THE VERY BASIC human desires is to feel a sense of belonging and connection. There is no reason that a place of work can't provide a tremendous sense of belonging. I'm sure you've heard people describe their co-workers as extended family. Let's strive to cultivate work environments that provide your employees with that sense of being part of something greater.

NAME TAGS

I saw this sense of belonging and connection in a very small example when I traveled to a Disney property for a conference. On all the employee name tags, in addition to their name it listed something they loved or felt passionate about such as fishing, travel, rescue dogs, classical music, and other interests. I observed rapport being made in several interactions including my own as guests and employees would bond over that immediate shared passion. It was such a simple way to create a connection through shared interests and strengthen a culture of belonging and kindness.

FISH GAME

In my **Economy of Kindness** program, I knew I wanted to bring in some gamification to teach my audience while they were having fun. Project Go Fish was the perfect game to make my point about an unkind work environment.

This is how the game is played:

Each table is covered with enough fish so that every participant could choose one of the four different colors: purple, green, yellow and blue. After participants chose their fish, they joined a "school" in one of the corners of the room that matched their fish.

Once the schools were assembled they were each given the rules: "Make friends with all the other fish. You must socialize, participate, communicate and contribute to Project GO FISH! Making your school of fish as you go along."

Ideally, the schools were to mingle with each other and when they made a connection, the participant could start a new school of multi-colored fish. Eventually, there would be many schools with assorted people trailing behind.

But the green, blue, and yellow fish had a secret instruction: Purple fish are dangerous! Avoid the purple fish at all costs! Making eye contact with the purple fish was deadly. They must not include purple fish in their school of fish under any circumstance.

Then the game would start. Watching this play out with dozens of audiences was fascinating. Within just a couple of minutes, you would see schools of fish avoiding those purple fish, moving around the room. I had a CEO of a company tell me she couldn't play the game. Once she heard the directions she sat out telling me, it felt like the opposite of being kind.

Usually it didn't take long for some of the purple fish to catch on, because they had a friend or colleague in a different group who was following the directions and avoiding including them in their school of fish.

The game only goes on for a couple of minutes and at the end we would debrief. I'd ask the purple fish, "How did that feel?" They almost always would say something like "Terrible!"

"Not fair." "I didn't like it." "Left out!" When I'd ask the other fish, "How did that feel for you?" most would say things like, "I didn't feel good about it." "I hated ignoring them, that was my boss, my friend . . ." "That felt awful."

Then I'd reveal why the purple fish had been ignored. I'd ask how they thought this correlates to the work environment. We discussed how a new employee could feel like that purple fish, or perhaps someone of a diverse background could feel ostracized if your company culture was not inclusive. The game brought out rich discussion about how excluded the purple fish felt and no matter where you stood in your company you could actually experience that discomfort during this Project Go Fish game.

At the end of the discussion, we'd all give the purple fish a big virtual hug and thank them for participating. It wasn't easy being the purple fish.

This soon became one of my absolute favorite parts of my program. I knew that the audience would gain insight about their organization and it seemed that doing it in this fun game setting was honestly one of the best ways to let them experience in an absolutely visceral way what an unkind workplace might feel like and how you might not even be aware that you are participating.

In May 2020, during the spring of the pandemic, when I did a virtual program for one of my past clients, I was absolutely thrilled when one of the participants put on a hat with a fish image she had created. It was rewarding to see the lasting effects the fish game had garnered.

BELONGING WITH BABY

A few years ago, when I was preparing for a conference of nurse practitioners, I interviewed my now all grown up kids' babysitter, Claire. When she left Oregon, she became an outpatient Nurse Practitioner of Vascular Surgery at a large hospital in Baltimore, Maryland. Even though she had been in Baltimore for almost a decade, she had often felt like an outsider. But that changed when her son was born at 25 weeks of gestation. She told me about a tremendous act of kindness from her colleagues.

The first thing was Claire's boss sent out an email to update her fellow employees about how she and her newborn son were doing. The response was stunning. Knowing that she was only allowed a few weeks of maternity leave, the staff donated more than 400 hours of PTO (Paid Time Off) for her which provided 10 weeks of uninterrupted pay.

It was a huge gift and Claire says, "When I received the notification of time off I was really in disbelief at the generosity of people in my overarching department. Not only had people in my specialty donated, but many people from different surgical specialties who I hardly knew had donated their hard earned time off. It made me feel so cared for, but also taught me a lesson that going forward I wanted to pass on generosity like this when I learned of people in need."

Claire also noted that when the nurses she worked with checked in on her after she was finally able to take her son home, she felt like she had formed some incredible relationships. Those follow up phone calls made Claire feel very cared for and supported.

INTERVENTION FOR LACK OF KINDNESS

As I began speaking to more organizations from a variety of professional industries, I was a little surprised the first time someone came up to me after my **Economy of Kindness** program and asked, "What do we do with someone who just isn't kind?"

Since I had never had this point blank inquiry before, I reached out to several Human Resources colleagues about it. They told me that of course, there could be official conversations and documentation about any disciplinary behavior but bottom line someone who is in an organization and repeatedly is unkind just might need to be fired. There is no question that there are just some people in this world who don't care or want to be kind.

That said, it has always been my belief that people who are mean or unkind, likely are hurt people. Perhaps they have been hurt by someone in their life and they just repeat that behavior as they live their lives. One antidote to this, at least for some of them, might be to "kill 'em with kindness." Take the time to learn a little about them, maybe allow them some time to be fully listened to. It is possible that you may actually be able to change their behavior.

We all know of a good movie or two where the mean person can be changed through love. I'm not sure those movies don't have a kernel of truth in the real world. Loving someone who is difficult is actually not all that easy, but can be very gratifying if you are able to soften that mean person through love and kindness. Anyway, I'd consider trying that before I'd fire someone, but you'll have to be the judge of what works best in your place of business.

EXPECTATIONS

What is the statute of limitations for saying thank you? During a presentation, I asked participants to think of a time when they had missed the mark on being kind to someone one else. Perhaps something had gotten in the way and I asked what they might do differently in the future.

One very honest attendee said, "A fellow employee filled in for me while I was on medical leave for over two months." Then she continued, "This person is a very challenging and difficult co-worker and even though she'd filled in for me, I find it very hard to engage with her, she often brushes people off when they interact with her." She finally sheepishly added, "I'm embarrassed to share that I never thanked her officially even though now I wish I had acknowledged her efforts."

Was it too late to say thank you? A month or two months after someone has helped you? Can you make a different choice if you are now aware that you aren't happy with the first choice? It is likely that because of the difficulties with this co-worker it was easy to just gloss over the help she'd given. But in sharing this with us, the attendee was still feeling grateful for the help she'd received and realized even though this is a challenging co-worker she does deserve the acknowledgement.

So, is it too late to say thank you now? Not at all. There is no statute of limitations on saying thank you. It takes some intestinal fortitude to do the right thing but it is rarely too late to try to rectify a wrong or acknowledge a right.

No one wants to be a purple fish. Everyone wants the opportunity to be connected to the greater community, even if they are a prickly fish.

17

Recognition

PEOPLE APPRECIATE HAVING their efforts recognized and acknowledged. Most of us will work even harder when that recognition comes from someone we respect and trust. Maintaining employee morale is simple when you find ways to acknowledge the hard and smart work of individuals and teams.

Very basic and informal recognition is when a manager looks for opportunities to praise employees. Catching people doing something right and publicly acknowledging it is inspiring for the other people who surround them.

The pandemic created job insecurity as would new ownership or a merger for an organization. During the pandemic employees were anxious to keep their jobs while keeping up with their workload. And if they were working remotely they had to improvise a work setting while managing new protocols, health requirements, technology challenges and sometimes being totally isolated or overwhelmed with people surrounding them and needing attention.

Employers and managers who recognized this very real struggle and allowed employees to share their challenges were acknowledging the difficulties and offering tremendous support to their employees.

Creating opportunities in groups and one on one meetings to talk about what else was going on besides work allowed employees a chance to feel closer and connected in a deeper human way with their co-workers and managers.

One team at a hospital in Minnesota made it their goal every other week to walk through the hospital to spread kindness. One week they bought support socks and put notes on them that said, "We Support You!" Another week they brought mints to all departments for "mask mouth." They shared pictures from community children with thank you messages and created pop up markets where employees could grab cheese, milk, bread and other items on their way out the door to go home. They also regularly shared single serving snacks for the healthcare workers to grab on the go. This support has been genuinely received and welcome from their employees.

During the isolation, some companies planned activities like a virtual book club or happy hour, to encourage employees to connect and hear from others helpful ideas to move successfully through this strange and uncertain time.

MEETINGS

Meetings are a perfect opportunity to help set the tone for your culture. Consider giving a shout out at the beginning of a team meeting to acknowledge an individual or team that has performed well. It always has to be genuine and honest. Beginning your meetings on a positive note can help set the tone of gratitude for all the work your employees do.

According to research by Harvard Business School Assistant Professor Ashley V. Whillans, published in an HBS Working Knowledge article in 2019, "More than 80 percent of American employees say they do not feel recognized or rewarded, despite the fact that US companies are spending more than a fifth of their budgets on wages." She goes on to say, "Among the happiest employees, 95 percent say that their managers are good at providing positive feedback."[1]

In fact, a simple, heartfelt "thank you" from a manager is often enough for employees to feel like their contributions are valued and will motivate them to try harder. To be most effective, the praise should be specific, highlighting the worker's unique contributions and it should be timely.

Tell the employee how they are valued before they announce they have a better offer from another company. Get creative to provide the recognition your team needs. One company uses video at their monthly meetings to give a 1-2 minute video shout out to an employee who has done something worthy of recognition that month. The next month, the employee keeps on the lookout to choose another employee to spotlight.

You can recognize your top employees through internal company wide and external industry wide newsletters, a press release for the local media, your reader board at the company entrance, or the bulletin board in the break room. Your goal is to have them acknowledged at the level of their contribution which also makes the company shine brighter.

FRIENDLY COMPETITION

A wonderful virtual receptionist company, headquartered in Portland, Oregon that I started hearing about in my workshops, called **Ruby Receptionist**, took this to the next level. They wanted to elevate and cultivate the kindness and happiness that their employees personally felt. One of the core values at Ruby is to foster happiness. They created a **21-Day Ruby Happiness Journal** which included some of the science about cultivating happiness as a choice that each of us can work towards every day.

The journal entries are simple: track three things you are grateful for today, one positive outward action you've taken, and one positive experience in the past 24 hours. The employees were to complete the journal for 21 days. Ruby added an incentive to encourage employees to participate.

At the end of the 21 days the names of employees who had completed their journals were entered into a raffle for a free trip to Hawaii with a companion.

They had an almost 100% participation rate. Why? Ruby had set up a win-win for their employees. They wanted them to participate because this is the prime value of their organization, they incentivized the behavior that they wanted anyway, and the result was positive on all accounts. They got participation and employees who were now engaged in a new habit of acknowledging gratitude.

SURPRISE & DELIGHT

It could be something simple and unplanned like bringing in some treats or coffee unexpectedly. If your company is working remotely, perhaps send your employees a thoughtful surprise. It could be a little succulent plant, chocolates, tea or coffee, aromatherapy, something that will bring delight and acknowledgement.

One of my clients sent a "package of sunshine." It was in a bright yellow envelope and all the items it contained were yellow like pineapple gum, chapstick, a bright yellow book about building a happiness mindset, and even a sunshine tinted hand sanitizer. This package was pretty special and definitely brought sunshine to their employees. The ideas for surprise and delight for your team are endless. You could organize a food cart to come to the office to provide lunch for everyone or organize an ice cream truck to arrive and buy everyone treats. Schedule an onsite massage therapist to visit your office to help alleviate stress during your busy season.

Surprise & Delight could also be given in time. An owner of a long-term care franchise told me that after 120 days of working remotely they finally returned to the office. Since it was summer, he opted to allow his employees to work remotely on Fridays and perhaps indefinitely. He told me that the decision was joyfully cheered by his employees. "It was like I'd given them an early Christmas present. We were all happy to come back to the office but also delighted to work remotely again on Fridays." His simple display of faith in their abilities was a tremendous gift for his team.

When you think about ways to bring **Surprise & Delight** for your employees, maybe think back to being a kid and receiving something that might have made you squeal with delight. If at all possible, create moments where you are able to do that for your employees as well.

One of my favorite kindness videos during the pandemic was shared at the end of August 2020 by the Detroit Tigers baseball franchise. It was just a one-minute video clip of the players receiving a surprise during batting practice, when their families were shown sending some wishes to their loved ones on the jumbotron.[2]

By that time the shortened baseball season was a month in. Many of the baseball players had been separated from their families for weeks. The expressions on their faces were absolutely priceless. The surprise and delight they were receiving was visible and we got to witness it in this brief video.

During the pandemic a simple act of kindness, such as getting a greeting from a loved one, was even more important. And this video showed exactly how these players felt by this incredible action their club had taken to boost them during this challenging time. Check out the one-minute video for yourself.

Another one of my absolute favorite stories during COVID-19 was complete surprise and delight. It happened in July, when a UPS driver named Hector Velasco started noticing a little boy hanging out on his balcony watching the UPS truck drive by every day. He could tell the boy looked sad. The next day, he left a note for the little boy's parents. It said, "Hi, this is Hector, your UPS driver. I've seen your son plenty of times on the balcony and he seems very sad [that] he doesn't get any packages." He left his phone number and the parents contacted him. The next day, Hector brought a "special delivery" box to the little boy. It was filled with race cars and candy. The picture of the little boy smiling ear to ear with the UPS driver waving behind him is absolutely priceless.[3]

I DON'T WANT RECOGNITION

Not everyone gets joy out of being publicly recognized and you need to respect that for your employees.

You can always acknowledge them privately in a phone call, an email, a handwritten note, a token of your appreciation, or a monetary reward.

When it comes to the person who is retiring from the company or just moving on to another department that would prefer no fanfare, you can still find ways to recognize their contribution to the company or the department privately and quietly. Keep in mind that they may be uncomfortable in the spotlight, being in large gatherings, or have other personal reasons for not wanting to make their transition a public display.

While your team may have preferred the party to pay homage to their colleague, encourage them to put their energy to use creating a keepsake book or video, selecting a memorable gift for the retiree, and to write a note to express themselves individually. Allow them to share some words or pictures or whatever else with the retiree and let them see the finished product but it can be delivered in a manner that isn't public so you are actually helping both the retiree get what they've requested but your employees do have that important closure.

Everyone has their preferences for recognition. One person may want a gift card for a restaurant while another would prefer one to the grocery store. Your job is to know your people well enough that you can deliver the type of recognition they would value.

Pro Tip:

Recognition is not just an acknowledgement of the employee but an incentive to keep performing well for the company. Here are some options for individual and group appreciation:

- **Spoken** — Manager looks to privately or publicly say "Well done!"

- **Written** — Thank you notes, bulletin boards, newsletter mention, outside reader boards, letters for employee files, and press releases

- **Monetary** — Gift cards, bonuses, salary increases

- **Professional Development** — Company paid attendance at conferences and seminars or online training and development, and in-house career development programs/mentorship

- **Gifts** — Company SWAG

- **Food** — Snacks, drinks, lunch, food cart, ice cream truck, popcorn machine

- **Workspace** — Improved or relocated, updated technology, access to additional resources

18

Why Does Kindness Matter Now More Than Ever?

THE OXFORD ENGLISH dictionary defines kindness as: the quality of being friendly, generous, and considerate. "She thanked them for their kindness and support."

A look at the definition of kindness seems that at our most basic level we should be able to achieve all of these behaviors; friendly, generous, and considerate. These should be innate human characteristics.

There is scientific evidence that doing kind deeds for another person boosts your serotonin, the chemical in our brains that helps create feelings of satisfaction and well-being. In addition, acts of kindness activate the parts of our brain associated with happiness, creating the experience known as a "giver's high."

Kindness is always a choice. Not only is it a choice, sometimes choosing kindness with others who are different than you leads to deep, rich, and unexpected relationships.

After the death of Justice Ruth Bader Ginsberg in 2020, many people learned about the long-standing friendship that Justices Ginsberg and Antonin Scalia (and their families) had for many years. Perhaps it was surprising to people that these two people who were very different politically, were able to have a strong and abiding friendship despite political conflicts.

The justices had opposing views, but they chose not to let that get in the way of first, their professional consideration of a topic, and second, their discovery of their shared interests like food, travel, and opera.

In a 2016 *New York Magazine* article, Justice Scalia described their lifetime appointment and friendship: "If you can't disagree ardently with your colleagues about some issues of law and yet personally still be friends, get another job, for Pete's sake."[1]

Ginsberg was known to have responded to a case differently after Scalia shared his "stinging dissent" before she was preparing her response. She would say that her response was better with time to consider his ideas properly. These were two brilliant minds with two very differing opinions who chose both professionally and personally to let their differences fuel their work and make them each better because of it. *Iron sharpens iron* comes to mind. These two human beings chose not to let their differing politics ruin a relationship with many more facets than the public perceived.

I have two speaker colleagues who have become unlikely friends. Jess and Meg met as roommates about nine years ago at our national speaker conference when both needed to save some cash on hotel accommodations. They were an unlikely match.

Meg called herself a mother of three with conservative leaning views. She is very active in her church. This first conference was a sort of vacation for her, a huge break from her responsibilities as a mom and an opportunity to begin to elevate her professional focus. For Jess, a queer outspoken super liberal west coaster whose work is about diversity and equity, these work conferences were the most important part of her professional development each year.

From the beginning their needs both at the conference and professionally seemed different. What they began to quickly realize was that each of them showed up granting themselves permission to not be perfect as "the mom" or "the professional" and in that space there was tremendous overlap.

In fact, both felt like they could be themselves, could learn about each other and different lifestyles, other people's choices, even opening up about why one or the other one had specific requests about something as simple as getting the cleaning service when they shared the room. Jess preferred not to get the service for a variety of reasons while Meg relished it since as a mom this felt like being pampered. When they learned why something was important to the other person it was much easier to find common ground.

Jess says she's realized, through her friendship with Meg, that she doesn't have to share 100% of everything and make someone as uncomfortable as physically possible to see if they trust her. That was a huge "aha."

Over the years their professional and personal relationship has deepened. They say they have endless subjects to talk about, they laugh so much when they are together, and neither remembers tiptoeing around any subject matter even at the beginning. Meg said, "If something came out of my mouth, I wouldn't feel tripped up." They gave each other the space of grace.

That first year of rooming together turned into many. They started an annual ritual at the beginning of each conference to order hamburgers to their room and touch base at the beginning of their stay each year. They have traveled to see each other.

Jess attended Easter with Meg one year and met her whole family, saying, "Since I was raised atheist, this was not an experience I was familiar with. I really appreciated the opportunity to fully participate if I wanted, but also to choose not to. It was cool and I felt comfortable." Their relationship has deepened as they built their trust in each other, knowing there is deep respect for the other person as a whole human being.

Meg says, "I'm inspired by Jess's openness. It's helped me in so many ways including changing how I introduced myself professionally."

When Meg was going through a challenging time a few years ago, Jess, who was speaking in the Midwest, drove a couple hours to drop off some flowers and check in. Jess says, "Meg has a good way of compartmentalizing her life, separating her personal and professional worlds and I wanted Meg to know we weren't just professional friends, but real friends."

Kindness and civility are always a choice. There will always be circumstances in our lives where we will meet people who are different from us. At the very basic level, choosing to behave civilly is incredibly important.

If it feels impossible to find common ground with someone, rather than letting the behavior become uncivilized, walk away and return later to the conversation when you are more in control to discuss sensitive subjects. We do have ways to build the tolerance and civility we want to create to live and work together.

When you can see past the differences, you may create an unexpected and beneficial relationship with someone who teaches you something that makes you a better person because of it.

19

Kindness In Other Traditions

HO'OPONOPONO

A FEW YEARS AGO, a friend shared a mantra inspired by Ho'opo-nopono, a Hawaiian practice of reconciliation and forgiveness. The mantra is: "I'm sorry, please forgive me, thank you, I love you." I had never heard of it and thought it was so beautiful and simple. This is an ongoing process to practice forgiveness. You can practice it both with others and with yourself.

Holding onto resentment towards others is harmful to the person who refuses to forgive. The Hawaiian word ho'oponopono comes from ho'o ("to make") and pono ("right"). The repetition of the word pono means "doubly right" or being right with both self and others. In a nutshell, ho'oponopono is a process by which we can forgive others to whom we are connected.

UBUNTU

A suburban lacrosse field may be an unusual place to first learn about this philosophy, but my son's coach used Ubuntu with the boys as a mantra for the team. Ubuntu "refers to a collection of values and practices that black people of Africa or of African origin view as making people authentic human beings."[1] While the nuances of Ubuntu vary across different ethnic groups in Africa, the Desmond Tutu Peace Foundation explains that in essence, Ubuntu can guide us all with its meaning of, "We are all connected. What affects one of us affects us all."[2]

More simply, my progress happens because of your progress. It means we can't be only for ourselves, we must be for the greater good. It is a reminder of how humans and society must treat each other. In the words of Desmond Tutu, "My humanity is bound up in yours, for we can only be human together."[3]

GEMILUT HASADIM

In Judaism, one of the more important mitzvah categories is doing acts of loving kindness, also called *gemilut chasadim*. The Talmud, a central Jewish text, says that *gemilut chasadim* is greater than *tzedakah* (charity), because unlike *tzedakah*, *gemilut chasadim* can be done for both the rich and poor, both the living and the dead, and can be done with our actions or with money.

This idea of a covenantal relationship between human beings means that we need to deeply understand the person at the other end of the giving cycle. According to the great 12th century Rabbi and Scholar Maimonides who created the Levels of Giving, the highest level of giving is to donate money, provide a loan, offer your time, or whatever else it takes to enable an individual to be self-reliant. I love teaching about Maimonides's levels of giving and Gemilut Hasadim because I believe these Jewish precepts call on our deep capacity for true kindness in the world.

Ladder OF GIVING
written by Maimonides, a 12th-century Jewish scholar

1 Giving money, a loan, your time, or whatever else it takes to enable an individual to be self-reliant.

2 Giving when neither the donor nor the recipient is aware of the other's identity.

3 Giving when you know who is the individual benefiting, but the recipient does not know your identity.

4 Giving when you do not know who is the individual benefiting, but the recipient knows your identity.

5 Giving before being asked.

6 Giving cheerfully and adequately but only after being asked.

7 Giving cheerfully but giving too little.

8 Giving begrudgingly and making the recipient feel disgraced or embarrassed.

CHEROKEE FOLK TALE

Everyone makes a choice on how they respond to their surroundings. This story reminds us to be conscious in our decisions.

• • •

A Cherokee man is teaching his grandson about life. "A fight is going on inside me," he said to the boy. "It is a terrible fight and it is between two wolves. One is evil — he is anger, envy, sorrow, regret, greed, arrogance, self-pity, guilt, resentment, inferiority, lies, false pride, superiority, and ego." He continued, "The other is good — he is joy, peace, love, hope, serenity, humility, kindness, benevolence, empathy, generosity, truth, compassion, and faith. The same fight is going on inside you — and inside every other person, too."

The grandson thought about it for a minute and then asked his grandfather, "Which wolf will win?" The grandfather simply replied, "The one you feed."

Every single one of us is welcome to live in this possibility if we simply begin to look for it. When the news is bleak and upsetting if that is all you focus on you will only see that misery exists. Instead, look around for the amazing generosity, kindness, and humility that surrounds you and feed on that.

20

Self-Care for Organizations

SELF-CARE IS TAKING care of your health and well-being so that you can manage your life, your relationships, and your job. Promoting self-care is a cost effective investment in your people which encourages them to maintain their mental and physical health so that they are able to perform at their best. Consider some of these self-care initiatives to lower the intensity of your workplace while maintaining productivity.

MANAGE MEETINGS

When you are convening a conference call, a video chat, or a gathering in the boardroom, ask yourself: "Is it necessary?" Meetings disrupt workflow and concentration whether they are necessary or not. When a meeting is required, respect everyone's time by having an agenda and starting and ending on time. Be kind and determine who really needs to attend and identify the shortest amount of time possible to accomplish your goal.

Do everything in your power to honor your employees' time. This might mean that meetings are scheduled more sparingly, kept shorter, or are limited to just one day a week. Meetings are often the reason people feel they aren't able to get their "real" work done. If it is possible to find a solution, make a plan, or distribute information in any other way without a meeting, do it.

Pro Tip:

Managers — If you have employees who are caregivers for children or parents, plan to start your important meetings after 9 a.m. and end before 4 p.m.

BOOK GROUPS

Along with team building, a book group is an opportunity to escape, relax and learn. As a self-care tool, having an excuse to dive into a book for a respite is just one of the benefits. By being part of a book group the readers get to exchange ideas and interact with colleagues they may not have encountered before. Now this can't be mandatory learning or it won't help anyone with self-care, but if it promotes learning and connection then it just might be beneficial.

TIME

Let's be honest. There is no such thing as work life balance. This was even more evident during the pandemic when employees' professional and personal lives were melded as they held down jobs in remote home worksites. Flexibility became one of the most important personal attributes of 2020.

Here are three ways you can provide opportunities for your teams to have additional time for self-care.

- ***Flexible hours*** is the first option. Talk to your employees and find out what would help them be most productive and also balance their lives. For example: starting work an hour later or earlier may solve transportation issues.

- *Autonomy* also allows for stronger self-care. Employees have proven that they can get the work done remotely, so allow them that autonomy to continue to do so. They'll be able to continue being a valued employee while managing their personal responsibilities with less duress.

- *Time off* is necessary. Do whatever you can to encourage your staff to take time off, let them know what time they have available to them, find creative ways they can take this time, and proactively encourage them to schedule it for themselves. If we live by the idea that we cannot serve from an empty tank we must find ways to help our employees re-fill their tanks!

Perhaps there are even unexpected opportunities to give your staff time off. Look through the calendar and find days of the year when you might be able to announce some unexpected time off. Google announced at the last minute that they were giving their employees the Friday before Labor Day off, calling it a 2020 "collective well-being" holiday. They told their employees, "Please take the time to do whatever you need for yourselves."

PERSONAL TOUCH

Prior to the pandemic, organizations brought in massage therapists for chair massages or nail technicians to give manicures and pedicures to their employees for some on-site self-care. Gift cards for haircuts, therapeutic massages, and spa treatments are great rewards and acknowledgements that tie into self-care.

WORKSPACE DECOR

During the pandemic, a woman working overseas for the U.S. Army had her entire desk area surrounded by plexiglass walls for social distancing. She wrote in a LinkedIn post that it made her feel like she was working in a fishbowl. So, she decorated her plexiglass with large colorful fish and ocean stickers. When life gives you lemons, make lemonade.

In terms of decorating a space, one way to provide self-care in a work environment is to add fresh flowers, lots of green plants, images of affirmations, or an inspirational print, and perhaps your yearly vision board. It's truly self-care to add anything that helps you feel inspired and uplifted every day in your space.

If you notice that an employee has a theme to their desk decor, this is a clue to finding the perfect gift when you have an opportunity to recognize their contribution to the company mission.

FOOD

Food is our most basic way to take care of ourselves and others. Frequently, we think about bringing in food (aka goodies) for celebrations and recognition, but don't underestimate the power of food as actual self-care.

When your employees are working extended hours or under other pressure to achieve a goal, providing nourishment ensures that they will have an opportunity for self-care. Order a lunch that goes beyond pizza and soda, arrange for a food truck to come and provide a fresh meal, or provide dinner to go so that it's one less thing to take care of at the end of a long day.

Think healthy and tasty and now you have some very deep and meaningful self-care going on for your staff. We make food when someone is in need, so think of ways to nourish your teams and give them self-care throughout the year.

SELF-CARE RESOURCES

Loving Kindness Meditation

Several years ago, I added a three-minute loving kindness section to my keynote program. I was nervous the first time I tried it. I wasn't a meditation teacher, but I'd been practicing it for a couple of years and found it had been helpful. I decided, while preparing for that program, that the world felt like it needed some extra loving kindness in that moment. The first time I led the exercise, it was a conference held in a huge banquet hall with close to 250 people. The meditation was brief but it was very powerful.

People often tell me that it is one of their favorite parts of my program. Even during the pandemic, when my programs were all virtual, offering loving kindness to my attendees was always beneficial and I was still often told afterwards it was one of their favorite exercises in my program.

If you aren't familiar with the Metta meditation. I suggest you look it up. It's a simple opportunity to close your eyes and give yourself a few minutes of guided mindfulness. I first learned about this from Sylvia Boorstein, a wonderful Buddhist teacher whose books and teachings I love.

Here is the meditation:

Let's begin.

Put away your pens and paper. Set your phone down. Get comfortable in your chair. Please uncross your legs and have both feet on the floor.

If you feel comfortable, close your eyes. Make sure you feel comfortable on your chair. Now, take a deep breath in and let it out.

Begin by thinking about someone you love immensely. It could be a parent, spouse, child or friend but someone who when you think about them makes you smile. Most people have more than one. Imagine just one for right now and imagine them right here in front of you.

I want you to send them this blessing in your mind. . .

May you be happy
May you be healthy
May you feel safe
May you live with ease

Now think about someone that you would recognize if you saw them in your daily activities. Someone who is familiar to you. Maybe you see them at the bank or the grocery store or in your neighborhood. Someone that you've probably never thought about but that you would recognize if you bumped into them out and about in your daily routine.

Think of this familiar stranger, and wish for them. . .

May you be happy
May you be healthy
May you feel safe
May you live with ease

Now take another deep breath in and let it out. Put your hands on your heart.

Feel yourself sitting here, sitting here surrounded by all of these people.

Feel yourself hopefully content at this moment.

Now, we are going to give ourselves some loving kindness.

Think in your mind this blessing for yourself. . .

May I be happy
May I be healthy

May I feel safe
May I live with ease

Before you open your eyes now, think of the people here with you today. Think of the person in front of you or behind you, someone on your left and right. Now let's radiate some loving kindness blessings to everyone here today. . .

May you be happy
May you be healthy
May you feel safe
May you live with ease

When you open your eyes now, look around. Look at the person on your right and on your left, across the table from you. Smile at everyone who has been blessing you.

It's a lovely feeling to receive blessings from everyone around us today.

COVERING YOUR BASES

During the fall of 2020, while participating on a Zoom call for parents of college age students, a Portland pediatrician shared a simple self-care technique created by the behavioral health team at Metro Pediatrics where she works. It's called **Covering Your BASEs**. She told us they often use this for their patients and families struggling with depression. It made a huge impact on me because it's simple to remember and implement.

BASE stands for:

- **Body** — What am I doing today for my body? Physical, spiritual, emotional — do something today to nourish your body. Eat well, get some fresh air, exercise, pray, meditate, pause, enjoy a refreshing shower or a relaxing bath. Read or listen to something that uplifts your spirits.

- **Accomplishments** — What am I accomplishing today? This doesn't have to be a huge accomplishment. Folding laundry, making a pot of soup or organizing a drawer counts as an accomplishment. She encouraged us to make a list with a checkbox and physically check it off every day once you complete the task. That physical action of checking the box signals that you have accomplished something and can make a difference in your wellbeing.

- **Social Connection** — Who am I connecting with today? Phone, text, FaceTime and Zoom. We have multiple ways to make sure we get social connections every day even if we can't physically visit with our varied connections.

- **Enjoy** — Do at least one thing you enjoy every single day. This could overlap with any of the actions you've taken for the previous letters. It's wonderful to enjoy something you have done for your body, your daily accomplishment, or that social connection you made. Just do one thing you enjoy today.

I include **Covering Your BASEs** in my **Economy of Kindness** programs because it is a quick, simple, and powerful reminder for self-care. Give it a try.

3 GOOD THINGS

This simple activity takes five minutes before bed. Write down three things you are grateful for that day. It literally takes less than five minutes but the research shows that by focusing on what we are grateful for, we will notice more of it.

If you try this exercise for just two weeks you will already begin to feel the effects. In fact, according to the study, a two-week trial of **3 Good Things** can have lasting benefits for up to six months.[1] Simply by acknowledging what we are grateful for each day we will increase our happiness and decrease depression. One healthcare organization prescribed this **3 Good Things** exercise rather than prescribing antidepressants. It's that effective.

Other results include:

- Reduced levels of burnout
- Better sleep quality
- Improvements with personal and professional relationships

Here's all you need to do. Place a small notebook or journal by your bedside and before you go to bed each night write down three things you are grateful for from the day. You could do it on your phone, but there is a physical connection when using pen and paper that apparently makes a stronger impact.

Give it a try for two weeks. Think of what you could gain!

THANK YOU & GRATITUDE LETTERS

Saying thank you to someone who has influenced your life is a magical opportunity. Years ago, when my kids were still in elementary school, I witnessed my daughter's fifth grade teacher receiving a letter from a student he'd had 25 years previously. The student's parents were divorcing the year she was in his class and she told him how his kindness as a solid adult has been something she's been grateful for ever since. She was finally writing to tell him. There were tears and I was blessed to witness what receiving that letter meant to one of our favorite teachers.

Think of someone who has meant something to you. It could be a friend, mentor, family member, coach, colleague, anyone whose kindness touched you deeply. It may even be someone you've lost touch with.

Sit down and write them a letter or note. Don't feel overwhelmed. If you only write a few sentences or a single paragraph it will be meaningful. Let them know what they did that you remember. Tell them how their kindness impacted you. Let them know how you've remembered this for however long it's been.

They may be surprised by your acknowledgement, delighted to hear they had a positive impact, and your note will perpetuate kindness.

21

Associations

ASSOCIATIONS & PROFESSIONAL KINDNESS

Our professional affiliations extend beyond our work environment as many of us are members of community, service, and business organizations. I attend a great deal of conferences as a keynote speaker. For me, a total extrovert, a conference can be a wonderful way to meet lots of interesting new people and get pumped up. But for others, having to make small talk and meet dozens of new people leaves them feeling drained rather than energized.

Extending kindness at business meetings, conferences, and seminars should be part of the initial planning and also something you can share as an individual to ensure everyone feels valued and recognized. Here are effective solutions for managing boards, membership, and events with kindness.

ON BOARDING

As the new president of my state chapter of the National Speakers Association, I asked my board to complete a little get to know you homework. Each person was asked to create an authentic introduction about themselves (two pages at the most) not their professional CV but their personal background, hobbies, family, and other details, plus three images that were important to them. The responses were compiled into a "Meet the Board" PDF, and I shared it with my board prior to our first retreat together.

This was a fun way to get to know the folks we'd be serving with beyond their professional resume. Give it a try if you want to have your volunteers get to know each other before they work together. You might be surprised at some of the overlapping details you'll learn about each other.

CREATING A CULTURE

Make it a practice, starting with your board members, when there's a newcomer in your midst to welcome them and show them the ropes, including providing a calendar and a job description for the post they are taking. Let them know who else on the board or within the membership can assist them with their tasks and check in regularly to ensure they are successful and comfortable.

By showing this kindness to your board, they are more likely to incorporate it into their dealings with members at meetings and those who volunteer to work on committees. You'll be planting seeds of compassion and support that will make your organization blossom.

ADDITIONAL WAYS TO WELCOME NEWCOMERS

Creating a good set of opportunities for newcomers is a lot like onboarding someone at a company. Think about all the ways you can create meaningful connections and successful integration into the association culture. This will set you up with potential members, volunteers, and board members for years to come.

- Create a special name tag to help identify first timers at your meeting or a conference and announce the identifier to the general membership. For conferences, include this information in your welcome package or conference schedule. This creates a conference culture that doesn't put all the responsibility on the new attendee.
- Anyone can welcome a newcomer whether it's their assignment or not. The distinctive name tag also helps first time attendees bond when they see each other and can identify that someone else is also a newbie.
- Depending on the size of your event and the schedule, announce and introduce the newcomers at the start of your meeting.
- At a conference, offer a first timer orientation session and a newcomers welcome event the first night as well. Finding a few familiar faces at the beginning of the conference can help newcomers feel like they have others just like themselves.
- Have a section of the room or special table(s) marked for newcomers at the first couple of meals so newcomers don't feel like everyone has a seat and they don't. Assign a board member to be the table captain.
- Identify and assign ambassadors, people who will look out for the newcomers, and ensure that they get a chance to meet other people and are integrated into the event.

Remember, your organization's culture is under scrutiny when a newcomer walks in. They want to be welcomed, involved, and recognized. If that happens then you will have a committed member.

Outreach

Maintaining contact with the membership of your organization makes them feel involved even when you are not able to meet. A newsletter lets them know what's going on and a Facebook page and website give them a way to reach out to each other as well between face-to-face gatherings.

During the global pandemic in 2020, all of our programs for our state NSA chapter had of course shifted to a virtual format and our board wanted to find a way to connect to our members.

At the start of the shutdown, we initiated a phone tree to touch base and leave a message for every member ensuring they were doing okay through the pandemic. In December 2020, we did a little self- care package, with lip balm, mints, granola bars, hand sanitizer, a bag of calming tea, and a packet of Emergen-C vitamin drink. We sent it in a bright blue package as a small gesture to let our members know we were all in this together. We did a second phone tree that month, too.

When you notice someone is missing from your regular meetings, or you've heard that they are having an especially stressful time, a friendly call from a board member can make a world of difference! We felt that extra effort to reach out during the pandemic was crucial.

Greeters and Registration

For years, and for a variety of organizations I have shared the value of having greeters to welcome people at an event. Whether you are at a week-long conference or a monthly meeting everyone loves to be greeted by a smiling knowledgeable person who guides you through the moments of disorientation.

Being a greeter is a crucial job at any successful event. Greeters should be positive, welcoming, and helpful. They need to have the most information about the event and the venue because they will be answering the most questions. Provide them with more information than you think they will need and they'll keep things running smoothly.

Personally, I love being a greeter. When I joined my first professional networking group, I volunteered to work at the registration table for the monthly meeting. My job was to register attendees, take payments, answer questions, and smile. It was a win-win for everyone. The group needed help with registration and I also met every single participant each month — talk about instant networking!

Around that same time, my children attended a wonderful summer arts day camp. As a member of the board, I learned that new families who were signing up to register their kids for the first time were feeling disoriented as they entered our camp. There was so much commotion going on with registration and sign in on those Monday mornings that it wasn't clear who they needed to speak to or what to do.

I volunteered to be a Monday morning greeter. I knew the protocol having been a parent at the camp for more than 10 years and thought I'd be able to help with some of the traffic flow on Monday mornings. It was an absolute joy. I answered questions, directed people to the right places, and was a smiling friendly addition to the harried registration crew. Personally, it was actually fulfilling for me as I often would see parents I knew from other parts of our lives from all over Portland and it was a lot of fun.

If I am any example, the right person for the right job can be beneficial to all parties involved. Or perhaps I also have an insatiable urge to be a greeter. Anyway, next time you need a greeter give me a holler!

Buddy System

If you've been to camp then you know that you always use the Buddy System when you do any activity like fishing, hiking, or swimming. The Buddy System provides a safety net especially for the inexperienced.

Several years ago, I attended my first National Speakers Association conference. I knew a few people because I am a member of our local chapter but with nearly 3,000 people in attendance, even I, a certified 100% extrovert, was feeling a bit overwhelmed when I arrived.

Fortunately, a few months before the conference, I'd been speaking with a professional colleague I had never met who lived in another city. When I mentioned that I'd be attending the conference for the first time, she offered to be my "Buddy."

The first night at the opening session we found each other, and I sat with her and a few colleagues she introduced me to. She even invited me out to dinner that first night with her cohort. She's an incredibly well-loved professional in our association so having had that one on one time turned out to be pretty special. Also, having her offer to be my Buddy provided incredible comfort to me. It helped me feel less alone in a sea of people I didn't know.

The year I served as president of our state chapter, my board and I made sure anyone attending their first annual conference felt very much included and knew what to expect throughout the event. I guess you could have called us the Big Buddies.

We even created a group text for folks who wanted to meet up for general sessions. Board members were assigned to find a table at each general session and text the group throughout the conference so people could always find familiar faces in a very large room if they wanted to. This helped many of those first timers feel included during the conference.

A Buddy System can really make a difference. Making that new member feel like they belong is a huge accomplishment for any organization. If your conference is too big to organize it on the national level, do it chapter to chapter or state to state, anything that helps break it down so it becomes possible to team up a Buddy with the newcomer.

Scholarships

Most companies have a professional development budget to encourage employees to attend conferences in support of their job. Frequently the associations hosting the events offer full or partial scholarships so that more people have the opportunity to attend.

One of the first years I attended our National Speakers Association annual conference, I was the recipient of a scholarship from our association. That year, my husband was going through cancer treatment and my business was struggling. I applied for a scholarship and knew I would use everything I learned back at the chapter level as I was also a new board member.

Our chapter hosts an event about a month after the conference, called **Stir the Paint**, where anyone who attends the conference can come and share with those who didn't attend. It's a great opportunity to distribute that newly learned information with our peers. Plus, as a recipient of a scholarship, this program allows them to share that professional knowledge even further.

The years I was President Elect and President, our chapter paid partial and fully for attendance at the national conference. I know this doesn't count as a scholarship, but it is a wonderful incentive to recognize your board leaders and get them exposure to the larger national organization in the years they are serving your chapter. The year I was president we had over 20 people in attendance at the national conference. Perhaps a part of that was my enthusiasm about the annual event and talking about it and the value it added to my own business.

The Fundraiser

The very first year I attended our National Speakers Association conference, I scraped together the money to get there. It wasn't cheap with the registration, travel, hotel etc. I knew it was important to invest in myself but truthfully I couldn't really afford it yet.

At the conference, there was a special fundraising event one of the evenings that required an extra ticket that cost $75. My graduate education was in fundraising so I enjoy these types of evenings, but since it had been such a stretch to get to the conference in the first place I hadn't purchased the additional ticket.

The morning of the fundraising event, I stopped by the registration booth thinking I might be able to volunteer to work the event. I presented my plan to the volunteer at the registration desk who unfortunately told me the only way to participate was to purchase my own $75 ticket.

Out of the blue, the woman standing next to me said, "I'd love to buy you a ticket so you can go." It was a crazy random act of kindness. She didn't know me, had never met me and had no idea what I spoke about either. It was an incredible gesture and one I've never forgotten. I haven't been able to buy anyone else's ticket yet to the fundraising event but I have been able to afford the fundraiser in the subsequent years since that first conference.

Again, consider that your new attendees might be newer in their businesses, not flush with cash. If there are any events like this that require an extra ticket fee, consider establishing a way to underwrite their tickets so they can attend and don't have to miss *anything* that first year due to funding.

Off-Site Dinner Networking Opportunities

For one of the evenings of your conference organize an off-site dinner for participants. Work with your host chapter or city to help organize a selection of local restaurants in different locations to dine near the conference site.

Choose different types of cuisine and different price ranges. If there is more than one popular restaurant with the same cuisine, no problem, you'll likely need it. Keep the reservations to not more than 15 spots at each restaurant and have the attendees sign up for whichever restaurant suits them not later than the day before the event.

Each group needs a restaurant host who will be a leader from your organization or a local member from the host chapter. Make sure everyone signs up with their name and cell phone number so the restaurant host can communicate with the group.

Once everyone is signed up, the restaurant host contacts their group to set the departure time and method to the restaurant. Dining with a random group of people means new connections and rich conversation as you break bread together and enjoy food that you all prefer. This is a wonderful way to make a larger conference more intimate and get to see something of the city outside of the conference venue. Perhaps it will be so popular that it becomes an annual event once you try it.

Acknowledging Your Volunteers

In 2019, I attended a winter conference in late February for my National Speakers Association. That weekend, I met a National Board member named Rochelle. As soon as she introduced herself, I recognized her name.

As part of her role on the national board of directors she had called me when I was serving as our state chapter president to thank me for my volunteer commitment. I didn't know her, but it meant a lot to be acknowledged and recognized for my own service to our association.

It was the first thing I thought of when I met her. I said, "Thank you for taking the time to make those calls." She was notably surprised and also delighted that I'd remembered and that the call had made a difference to me.

I was thanking her as the recipient of her kindness. We all need to find ways to thank our volunteers for their efforts to keep our organizations vibrant and viable. Consider the options for honoring your association volunteers:

Awards ceremonies, celebration dinners, conference or travel stipend, "thank you" happy hour, thank you video from members, a legacy event or scholarship named after them, a small gift in their room at the annual conference, opportunities for professional development in their role, or a donation in their honor to a beloved charity. There are countless ways to tell someone they are appreciated. It is up to us to find the time and method to make sure they are acknowledged.

Using a Microphone

As a professional speaker, I always prefer to use a microphone to protect my voice and so I can be heard by everyone. Repeatedly, I've seen so many people at meetings or conferences who aren't professional, who have to speak in front of a group to ask or answer a question, or to participate in a discussion say, "I don't need to use the microphone. You can hear me right?" The correct answer is "No! We can't!"

These people shy away from the microphone because **they** are uncomfortable speaking into it. But **someone** in the audience won't be able to hear them without the microphone.

As speakers we say, "It's not about me, it's about my audience." So despite feeling nervous, please always make sure as the organizer of an event, when someone is speaking or asking a question that they always use the microphone. That way everyone can listen and hear what they have to say.

22

A Future Of Kindness

MY PERFECT WORLD OF the future seen through a lens of kindness would be more like a kindergarten class. At that age, children hug each other and hold hands, they laugh, sing, dance and play. They don't see each other's differences, they see each other as playmates to explore life with, to engage in make believe, and to spread joy. In my world, we would all be more childlike.

For the past several years I have wanted to write a book to share the valuable lessons in kindness that I learned from my audiences.

While cultivating kindness is considered an "evergreen" topic, meaning it will always be important and relevant, I'm aware that I have written this book at a unique and specific point in time in our world history.

As this book goes to press, the global pandemic continues. It has been a reset for the world and an opportunity for each of us to reexamine our lives and to see the cracks in our systems. Our eyes have been opened to the unquestionable inequity in healthcare, education and the justice systems in our country and around the world. We get it now, even if we haven't "lived" it that we must advocate for change.

At this particular moment in time we can carefully choose the way in which we move forward in our lives. Kindness, compassion, empathy, and civility are all choices. Even in the most difficult of situations, we have all heard of someone choosing kindness when they have been treated badly and could have just as easily chosen anger or hatred.

The choice of kindness is ours. As we offer it we should also expect it, even demand it from our companies, our media, and each other. We can reach across the table, the aisle, or the cubicle to begin to see each person as a valuable human being with their own gifts and challenges. These people may not look like you or have the same beliefs as you and yet they still deserve and desire kindness. Be willing to offer a listening ear, patient understanding, and the opportunity to find our commonalities rather than our differences.

I have been called a Pollyanna once or twice and I am 100% okay with that, because I choose to be the joy spreader, the energy lifter, the kindness sharer. I can tell you that it's not an easy job in a world set on spreading fear, anxiety and ridicule. I give you permission to join my mission and to be fearlessly kind; to be an authentic, vulnerable, heart centered leader, manager, or employee. You always have a choice to select kindness as your default setting.

I give you the power, right now, to become a kindness catalyst. Don't wait. Set this book down and share your gifts, your passion, your time, or your helpful wisdom with everyone in your orbit. Remember, it doesn't have to be something big, a small act of kindness has a ripple effect and spreads well beyond the initial recipient.

Just start looking. Begin a daily search to uncover the small simple ways you can make a difference through kindness. And if you need some guidance, support, or just want to share the joys of kindness you have discovered, I'd love to hear from you.

I hope this book will serve as a guidepost. That the stories, ideas, and suggestions I have made will be reminders for how to lead with kindness and generosity for your teams or organizations. Thanks for reading. May your days be filled with kindness.

Endnotes

Introduction

1. Samantha Swindler, "Good Samaritan Fired from U.S. Bank Gets New Job with Credit Union," *The Oregonian/OregonLive*, February 21, 2020, sec. Oregon News, https://www.oregonlive.com/news/2020/02/good-samaritan-fired-from-us-bank-gets-new-job-with-credit-union.html.

2. "Kindness 101 with Steve Hartman," *CBS News*, 2021, https://www.cbsnews.com/feature/kindness-101-steve-hartman/.

3. "SomeGoodNews," YouTube channel, YouTube, accessed May 31, 2021, https://www.youtube.com/channel/UCOe_y6KKvS3PdIfb9q9pGug.

4. "Hilton, American Express Offering One Million Hotel Rooms to Medical Professionals," *NBC12*, April 7, 2020, https://www.nbc12.com/2020/04/07/hilton-american-express-offering-one-million-hotel-rooms-medical-professionals/.

5. David Slotnick, "JetBlue Is Giving Away Free Flights to 100,000 Healthcare Workers — Here's How to Nominate Someone," *Business Insider*, May 6, 2020, https://www.businessinsider.com/jetblue-healthcare-workers-free-flights-flyover-2020-5.

6. Alyssa Newcomb, "Gap, Zara Start Producing Masks and Other Supplies for First Responders," *TODAY*, March 23, 2020, https://www.today.com/style/hanes-zara-start-producing-masks-other-supplies-first-responders-t176595.

7. "Captain Sir Tom Moore: 'National Inspiration' Dies with COVID-19 — BBC News," *BBC News*, February 2, 2021, https://www.bbc.com/news/uk-england-beds-bucks-herts-55881753#.

8. Jeryl Brunner, "25 Heartwarming Acts of Kindness Sparked by Coronavirus — Good News Stories," *Parade*, May 18, 2020, sec. Resolution Kindness, https://parade.com/1030288/jerylbrunner/coronavirus-good-news-heartwarming-stories/.

9. The Telegraph, *Heartwarming Moment D-Day Veteran Tears up as He's given a Pillow with a Picture of His Wife on It*, 2020, https://www.youtube.com/watch?v=UFubLKdO10k.

David Williams, "A Couple Left a $9,400 Tip at a Houston Restaurant to Help Staff Get through Coronavirus Shutdown," *CNN*, March 23, 2020, https://www.cnn.com/2020/03/17/us/houston-restaurant-coronavirus-tip-trnd/index.html.

10. Sydney Page, "A 9-Year-Old and Her Friends Raised $40,000 for Black-Owned Businesses by Selling Homemade Bracelets," *Washington Post*, June 8, 2020, https://www.washingtonpost.com/lifestyle/2020/06/08/9-year-old-girl-her-friends-raised-40000-black-owned-businesses-by-selling-homemade-bracelets/.

11. Sonja Lyubomirsky, *The How of Happiness: A New Approach to Getting the Life You Want*, Illustrated edition (New York, N.Y.: Penguin Books, 2008).

Foreword

1. Lyubomirsky.

2. Lara B. Aknin et al., "Prosocial Spending and Well-Being: Cross-Cultural Evidence for a Psychological Universal" (Harvard Business School, 2010), https://www.hbs.edu/ris/Publication%20Files/11-038_0f1218f0-91b3-4bae-8054-0fca25be5736.pdf.

3. "Americans Rate Kindness as Top Factor in Care," Dignity Health, November 13, 2013, https://www.dignityhealth.org/about-us/press-center/press-releases/majority-of-americans-rate-kindness.

4. Stephen J. Dubner, "How Do You Cure a Compassion Crisis?," Freakonomics Radio, December 16, 2020, https://freakonomics.com/podcast/compassionomics/.

5. Dubner.

Chapter 1 Culture

1. Tony Hsieh, *Delivering Happiness: A Path to Profits, Passion, and Purpose*, 1st edition (Grand Central Publishing, 2010).

2. Mike Rogoway, "Les Schwab Sold to California Investment Fund, Meritage Group," *The Oregonian/OregonLive*, September 29, 2020, https://www.oregonlive.com/business/2020/09/les-schwab-sold-to-california-hedge-fund-meritage-group.html.

3. Taylor Soper, "Tony Hsieh, Former CEO of Zappos Who Sold Online Shoe Retailer to Amazon for $1.2B, Dies at 46," *GeekWire*, November 28, 2020, https://www.geekwire.com/2020/tony-hsieh-former-ceo-zappos-sold-online-shoe-retailer-amazon-dies-46/.

4. "Rewriting the Rules for the Digital Age: 2017 Deloitte Global Human Capital Trends," Deloitte Global Human Capital Trends (Deloitte University Press, 2017), 110, https://www2.deloitte.com/content/dam/Deloitte/global/Documents/About-Deloitte/central-europe/ce-global-human-capital-trends.pdf.

Chapter 2 Feedback

1. Eleanor Singer, "The Use and Effects of Incentives in Surveys" (National Science Foundation, Washington DC, October 3, 2012), https://pdfs.semanticscholar.org/8c9f/fbdd8254a8d2cca67e258a52d7e0ac4570e6.pdf.

Chapter 3 Kindness in Customer Service

1. Kristin Marquet, "Author Laurie Guest: 'Here Are 5 Ways To Create a Wow! Customer Experience,'" *Authority Magazine*, February 2, 2020, https://medium.com/authority-magazine/author-laurie-guest-here-are-5-ways-to-create-a-wow-customer-experience-a037f3bc9cba.

2. Marquet.

3. Marquet.

4. The website Quote Investigator suggests that Carl W. Buehner can be credited with this adage. Many people have used the saying without ascription and the attribution to Maya Angelou is unsupported at this time: "They May Forget What You Said, But They Will Never Forget How You Made Them Feel," *Quote Investigator* (blog), April 6, 2014, https://quoteinvestigator.com/2014/04/06/they-feel/.

5. Shawn Achor, *Before Happiness: The 5 Hidden Keys to Achieving Success, Spreading Happiness, and Sustaining Positive Change* (New York: Crown Business, 2013).

6. Achor.

7. Achor.

Chapter 4 Kindness for Leaders

1. Brandon Laws, "The New Rules of Employee Experience and Communication in 2021," Transform Your Workplace, January 27, 2021, https://www.xeniumhr.com/blog/podcast/victoria-dew-new-rules-of-ee-engagement/.

2. Sheryl Sandberg and Adam Grant, *Option B: Facing Adversity, Building Resilience, and Finding Joy*, Illustrated edition (New York: Alfred A. Knopf, 2017).

3. "New Research by ATD: Mentoring Helps Employees and Leads to Better Business," Association for Talent Development, accessed May 31, 2021, https://www.td.org/press-release/new-research-by-atd-mentoring-helps-employees-and-leads-to-better-business.

4. Vineet Chopra and Sanjay Saint, "6 Things Every Mentor Should Do," *Harvard Business Review*, March 29, 2017, https://hbr.org/2017/03/6-things-every-mentor-should-do.

Chapter 5 Communication

1. Shawn Tully, "'The Crisis We Share': How Marriott CEO Arne Sorenson Turned Personal Tragedy into Collective Perseverance," *Fortune*, February 16, 2021, https://fortune.com/2021/02/16/arne-sorenson-ceo-marriott-dies-pancreatic-cancer/.

Chapter 7 Creating Mindfulness

1. Jane Murcia, "Hope in Unity and Kindness: Stress-Relief Station Offers a Safe Space for Frontline Providers," UCLA Health, April 15, 2020, https://connect.uclahealth.org/2020/04/15/hope-in-unity-and-kindness-stress-relief-station-offers-a-safe-space-for-frontline-providers/.

Chapter 8 Autonomy

1. Daniel Wheatley, "Autonomy in Paid Work and Employee Subjective Well-Being," *Work and Occupations* 44, no. 3 (August 1, 2017): 296–328, https://doi.org/10.1177/0730888417697232.

Chapter 9 Burnout

1. "Job Burnout: How to Spot It and Take Action," Mayo Clinic, November 20, 2020, https://www.mayoclinic.org/healthy-lifestyle/adult-health/in-depth/burnout/art-20046642.

2. "Workplace Burnout Survey | Deloitte US," Deloitte United States, accessed May 31, 2021, https://www2.deloitte.com/us/en/pages/about-deloitte/articles/burnout-survey.html.

3. Leslie Kane, MA, "Medscape US and International Physicians' COVID-19 Experience Report: Risk, Burnout, Loneliness," Medscape, September 11, 2020, https://www.medscape.com/slideshow/2020-physician-covid-experience-6013151.

4. Jennifer Moss, "Burnout Is About Your Workplace, Not Your People," *Harvard Business Review*, December 11, 2019, https://hbr.org/2019/12/burnout-is-about-your-workplace-not-your-people.

5. Moss.

6. Stephen Trzeciak and Anthony Mazzarelli, *Compassionomics*, 1st edition (Pensacola, FL: Studer Group, 2019).

Chapter 10 Being the Kindness Catalyst

1. Matt Crossman, "Forever Herb: The Laughs, the Leadership, the Legacy," *Southwest: The Magazine*, March 2019, https://issuu.com/southwestmag/docs/march2019/14.

2. Crossman.

3. Gary Kelly, "A Legacy of Love," *Southwest: The Magazine*, March 2019, https://issuu.com/southwestmag/docs/march2019/14.

Chapter 11 Reputation

1. Dara Kerr, "Uber CEO Dara Khosrowshahi Is Working to Clean House in Travis Kalanick's Wake," *CNET*, April 27, 2018, https://www.cnet.com/news/ubers-u-turn-how-ceo-dara-khosrowshahi-is-cleaning-up-after-scandals-and-lawsuits/.

2. Kerr.

3. Kerr.

4. Kerr.

5. Swindler, "Good Samaritan Fired from U.S. Bank Gets New Job with Credit Union."

6. "Response to the Recently Publicized Employment Decision," U.S. Bank, February 7, 2020, https://www.usbank.com/newsroom/stories/response-to-the-recently-publicized-employment-decision.html.

Chapter 12 Recruitment

1. Hsieh, *Delivering Happiness*.

Chapter 13 Retention

1. Heather Boushey and Sarah Jane Glynn, "There Are Significant Business Costs to Replacing Employees," Center for American Progress, November 16, 2012, https://www. americanprogress.org/issues/economy/reports/2012/11/16/44464/there-are-significant-business-costs-to-replacing-employees/.

2. "The Cost of Replacing an Employee and the Role of Financial Wellness," *Enrich* (blog), accessed June 1, 2021, https://www.enrich.org/blog/The-true-cost-of-employee-turnover-financial-wellness-enrich.

3. Ash Spiegelberg, "The Cloud Nine Culture," *Brunswick Review*, November 6, 2017, https://www.brunswickgroup.com/southwest-airlines-i6401/.

4. Justin Bachman, "Southwest to Avoid First Layoffs as Relief Bill Clears," *Bloomberg*, December 28, 2020, https://www.bloomberg.com/news/articles/2020-12-28/southwest-air-to-avoid-first-layoffs-as-relief-package-clears.

Chapter 14 Team Building

1. This quote is often attributed to anthropologist Margaret Mead, but no authoritative source can be found to support that attribution. The website

Quote Investigator examined how the saying has evolved and been attributed to different people over time: "Always Remember That You Are Absolutely Unique. Just Like Everyone Else," *Quote Investigator* (blog), November 10, 2014, https://quoteinvestigator.com/2014/11/10/you-unique/.

2. "2020 Cremation & Burial Projects Cremation Rate of 87% by 2040," National Funeral Directors Association, July 6, 2020, https://nfda.org/news/in-the-news/nfda-news/id/5223/2020-cremation-burial-projects-cremation-rate-of-87-by-2040.

Chapter 15 Legacy

1. Although this quote is often attributed to Mahatma Gandhi, no authoritative source can be found to support that attribution. The website Quote Investigator examined the history of a similar quote and suggested that the saying has evolved over many decades and cannot be attributed to a single individual: "Watch Your Thoughts, They Become Words; Watch Your Words, They Become Actions," *Quote Investigator* (blog), January 10, 2013, https://quoteinvestigator.com/2013/01/10/watch-your-thoughts/.

Chapter 17 Recognition/Acknowledgement

1. Dina Gerdeman, "Forget Cash. Here Are Better Ways to Motivate Employees," *Working Knowledge*, January 28, 2019, http://hbswk.hbs.edu/item/forget-cash-here-are-better-ways-to-motivate-employees.

2. "Tigers Get Surprise Messages from Family on the Big Board during Practice," *WXYZ*, August 26, 2020, sec. Sports, https://www.wxyz.com/sports/tigers-get-surprise-messages-from-family-on-the-big-board-during-practice.

3. "UPS Driver Surprises Boy with Special Delivery," ABC7 Los Angeles, July 19, 2020, https://abc7.com/6324683/.

Chapter 18 Why Does Kindness Matter Now More than Ever?

1. Chas Danner, "How the Republican Plan to Replace Justice Scalia Could Backfire," *Intelligencer*, February 14, 2016, https://nymag.com/intelligencer/2016/02/gops-plan-to-replace-scalia-may-backfire.html.

Chapter 19 Kindness in Other Traditions

1. Jacob Rugare Mugumbate and Admire Chereni, "Editorial: Now, the Theory of Ubuntu Has Its Space in Social Work," *African Journal of Social Work* 10, no. 1 (April 23, 2020), https://www.ajol.info/index.php/ajsw/article/view/195112.

2. "OUR MISSION + VISION," Desmond Tutu Foundation USA, accessed June 5, 2021, http://www.tutufoundationusa.org/mission-vision/.

3. "10 Pieces of Wisdom from Desmond Tutu on His Birthday," Desmond Tutu Foundation USA, October 7, 2015, http://www.tutufoundationusa.org/2015/10/07/10-pieces-of-wisdom-from-desmond-tutu-on-his-birthday.

Chapter 20 Self-Care for Organizations

1. Karin Rippstein-Leuenberger et al., "A Qualitative Analysis of the Three Good Things Intervention in Healthcare Workers," *BMJ Open* Volume 7 (May 2, 2017), https://doi.org/10.1136/bmjopen-2017-015826.

Resources

Cohen, Linda. *1,000 Mitzvahs: How Small Acts of Kindness Can Heal, Inspire, and Change Your Life.* New York: Seal Press, 2011.

Cohen, Linda. *The 1000 Mitzvahs Project: Linda Cohen at TEDx-CrestmoorParkWomen.* TEDxTalks. Denver, CO, 2012, https://www.youtube.com/watch?v=lxqjMpWosP4.

Nonfiction books on kindness:

Harding, Kelli. *The Rabbit Effect: Live Longer, Happier, and Healthier with the Groundbreaking Science of Kindness.* Reprint edition. New York: Atria Books, 2019.

Kraft, Houston. *Deep Kindness: A Revolutionary Guide for the Way We Think, Talk, and Act in Kindness.* Illustrated edition. New York: Tiller Press, 2020.

Lady Gaga. *Channel Kindness: Stories of Kindness and Community.* New York: Feiwel and Friends, 2020.

Mackesy, Charlie. *The Boy, the Mole, the Fox and the Horse.* Illustrated edition. New York: HarperOne, 2019.

Trzeciak, Stephen, and Anthony Mazzarelli. *Compassionomics.* 1st edition. Pensacola, FL: Studer Group, 2019.

Zaki, Jamil. *The War for Kindness: Building Empathy in a Fractured World.* New York: Crown, 2019.

Nonfiction books on happiness:

Achor, Shawn. *Before Happiness: The 5 Hidden Keys to Achieving Success, Spreading Happiness, and Sustaining Positive Change*. New York: Crown Business, 2013.

Hsieh, Tony. *Delivering Happiness: A Path to Profits, Passion, and Purpose*. 1st edition. New York: Grand Central Publishing, 2010.

Lyubomirsky, Sonja. *The How of Happiness: A New Approach to Getting the Life You Want*. Illustrated edition. New York: Penguin Books, 2008.

Nonfiction books on customer service:

Guest, Laurie. *The 10¢ Decision: How Small Change Pays Off Big*. Rolling Meadows, IL: Windy City Publishers, 2019.

ORGANIZATIONS

Random Acts of Kindness Foundation | www.randomactsof-kindness.org | The mission of The Random Acts of Kindness Foundation is to make kindness the norm® in schools, workplaces, homes & communities. They work toward that goal by creating free content that promotes kindness toward others & teaches important social emotional learning skills to kids. All of their resources are free.

Bounce Back Project | https://www.bouncebackproject.org | The Bounce Back Project™ is a unique collaborative of physicians, nurses, hospital leaders, staff and community partners in Wright County, MN, who have come together for a single purpose — to impact the lives of individuals, communities, and organizations by promoting health through happiness.

Born This Way Foundation | https://bornthisway.foundation | Co-founded and led by Lady Gaga and her mother, Cynthia Germanotta, Born This Way supports the mental health of young people and works with them to create a kinder and braver world. Through high impact programming, youth led conversations and strategic, cross-sectoral partnerships, we aim to make kindness cool, validate the emotions of young people, and eliminate the stigma surrounding mental health.

The Greater Good Science Center | https://greatergood.berkeley.edu | The Greater Good Science Center studies the psychology, sociology, and neuroscience of well-being, and teaches skills that foster a thriving, resilient, and compassionate society.

CNN "The Good Stuff" | https://www.cnn.com/specials/us/the-good-stuff | Every Saturday, they deliver stories of fascinating discoveries, everyday heroes, inspiring movements and great things happening right in your backyard.

Rotary International | https://www.rotary.org | Rotary provides service to others, promotes integrity, and advances world understanding, goodwill, and peace through fellowship of business, professional, and community leaders.

10 Ways Businesses Can Promote More Kindness

1. Encourage your employees to send thank you notes to each other — have thank you notes in the break room.

2. Have a kindness box. When an employee notices a kind act done by a colleague they stick it in the box. At the end of the month, acknowledge the employee with the most kind actions with a reward.

3. Create "gotcha" forms for your clients to fill out on behalf of your employees — if a client witnesses a kindness from an employee they can offer their feedback.

4. Create a baseline culture that everyone is doing the best they can at the moment. Reminds me of the saying: "Be kind, for everyone you meet is fighting a battle you know nothing about." — Ian Maclaren (disputed origin)

5. Share all the good news as well as the bad news — helps employees feel part of something that experiences both.

6. Newsletter or Meeting Recognition — Promote the culture you'd like to create by publicly recognizing the employees or volunteers who are getting mentioned by clients or their fellow employees. I read a story once in a newsletter where the volunteer said, "Don't underestimate the value of recognition. Even an "old-timer" volunteer like me can be moved and elevated by some unexpected recognition."

7. Promote: World Kindness Day November 13th, Random Acts of Kindness Day February 17th, Giving Tuesday (Tuesday after Thanksgiving), and choose other days throughout the year that have a similar theme to promote your culture of kindness and encourage employees to acknowledge them.

8. Volunteer Days of Service — Find local organizations that need help and organize a volunteer day together with fellow employees. Choose a day quarterly to organize service opportunities or other kindness themed giving days.

9. Recycling Programs — Bring awareness to your office by promoting a recycling program.

10. Kindness Corner — Create an interactive place where employees can share publicly a kindness that someone has done for them. Maybe use a chalk board in a lunchroom, or a white board in a hallway. Think of what an elementary school might do and copy that.

Acknowledgements

I am ever grateful to the people in my life who helped encourage, support, and envision the possibilities of this kindness work these past several years. There is rarely a direct path to create a new business. To find your voice and hone your message in the speaking business especially requires input and insight from others.

To my NSA Oregon colleagues Kevin McCarthy, Allison Clarke, and Jan Carothers, your vision and belief in my work have helped me overcome imposter syndrome on more than one occasion. Thank you for encouraging me to imagine the possibilities in my own business.

To my fellow NSA Board members, it has been a joy working together to serve our Oregon speakers community. I wouldn't be where I am today without the camaraderie and servitude so many of you have shared.

To the NSA Jewish Havurah group, our monthly Zoom calls during the pandemic were a lifeline. Thank you for allowing me to keep us on track and for all your kindness throughout. To Susan Friedmann, thank you for helping me navigate the publishing jungle.

To Zack Demopoulos and Deborah Walls, two of my favorite conference attendees ever. You are who every speaker dreams to have in their audience!

To Candy Whirley and Holly Hoffman, my two dear speaker pals. Thank you for all of the conversations we've shared during the pandemic. Your constant encouragement, support, love and belief in all that's possible were an absolute gift. Not only did we make it through the pandemic, we thrived!

To Jennifer Strait, my shaman and friend. I am deeply grateful for your guidance and advice always.

To Renee Spears, I can't even believe how much evolving has taken place in the years since we first met. You are a vision provider, an abundance creator, and a seed planter. Thank you.

To Pam Mack, you are a consummate connector. Thank you for your support and encouragement over the years. I'm so proud to also call you a friend.

To Rena Whittaker, thanks for giving me some of my earliest professional speaking and coaching opportunities. Angels at 10:10.

To Susan Finch, my friend, neighbor and fellow joy spreader. I'm grateful for your friendship and for your introduction to Nina Hambleton. Thank you Nina for all the hard work you do behind the scenes to help me look good out there.

To Julie Bond, my wonderful hairdresser! You found or created last minute appointments for me on more than a few occasions before speaking events and television appearances. Thank you for always making me look and feel my best.

To Julie Lucas, thank you for your incredible graphic work and always envisioning new ideas for the business. Love collaborating with you.

To Kim Rosenberg, your friendship has always been a tremendous gift to me. Thank you for being an unwavering cheerleader along the way.

To Jane Maulucci and Michael LaRocca, thank you for your keen eyes and great suggestions. I know my book is better because of your masterful editing skills.

To Nina Byrd, Claire Hanway, Leah Silbert, Victoria Dew, Brandon Laws, Karen Snyder, Laurie Guest, Jess Pettit, and Meg Bucaro Wojtas, thank you for letting me include your ideas, stories, or our conversations in this book.

To my children, I love you both deeply. To Gabrielle, you are strong willed, talkative and insightful and have taught me so much both as a mother and professional working woman. To Solomon, your thoughtful quiet nature has taught me (and still teaches me) about trying to sit in silence to allow you to share your wisdom. I am honored to be your mother as you both gallop into adulthood.

To my husband Aaron, you've been misunderstood by others, but together we have enjoyed the true unfolding of our innate gifts. I love your intelligence, integrity, and your heart. Thank you for seeing in me what I haven't always seen in myself. I love you.

ABOUT THE AUTHOR

Linda Cohen, also known as the Kindness Catalyst, has been a nationally recognized kindness expert and professional speaker for over a decade. Cohen works with a wide variety of businesses and associations on the ROI of Kindness. Her first book, 1,000 Mitzvahs: How Small Acts of Kindness Can Heal, Inspire and Change Your Life, was published in 2011 by Seal Press. Cohen's highly interactive style will engage your attendees, boosting their morale, while sharing "aha" insights and tips to help navigate change.

She served as president of the National Speakers Association Oregon Chapter in 2019. Cohen received her BA from American Jewish University and an MA from Brandeis University. Originally from New England, she now resides in Oregon with her husband of 28 years. They have two spirited young adult children, Gabrielle and Solomon, and two Cavalier King Charles Spaniels, Ginger and Remy. She loves practicing yoga and meditation and will never pass up a good cup of Earl Grey tea.

Contact Linda:
www. lindacohenconsulting. com

Made in the USA
Middletown, DE
04 October 2021